North American Short Stories

North American Short Stories
Book 2

Robert M. Stevenson
Jane L. Stevenson

NELSON

Thomas Nelson and Sons Ltd.
Lincoln Way Windmill Road
Sunbury-on-Thames Middlesex

P.O. Box 73146 Nairobi Kenya

Thomas Nelson (Australia) Ltd.
19-39 Jeffcott Street West Melbourne Victoria 3003

Thomas Nelson and Sons (Canada) Ltd.
81 Curlew Drive Don Mills Ontario

Thomas Nelson (Nigeria) Ltd.
8 Ilupeju By-pass PMB 1303 Ikeja Lagos

Copyright © 1976   Robert M. and Jane L. Stevenson
First publsihed 1976
Reprinted 1979

ISBN 0 17 555096 4

Printed in Hong Kong

Acknowledgments

The adaptations of the following stories included in this book
are published by special arrangement with the United States
Information Agency, Washington, D.C.

"The Bride Comes to Yellow Sky" and "The Blue Hotel"
by Stephen Crane, adapted by Mary Jeanne Blough, from *The
Red Badge of Courage and Other Stories,* a Ladder Classic
Edition published by Popular Library, Inc. Copyright 1965.

"Love of Life" by Jack London, adapted by Annette P.
Kane, from *To Build a Fire and Other Stories,* a Ladder
Edition, published by Popular Library, Copyright 1967.

All of the Exercises are the original work of the authors.

Contents

Introduction

The exercises in this book were prepared for intensive reading practice. This means that the student must read and prepare each assignment thoroughly and carefully at home, paying particular attention to vocabulary and the structures in which this vocabulary is contained.

The format of the exercises is, for the most part, the same for all lessons. The first exercise presents multiple-choice questions which the student can answer correctly only if he has read the selection with care.

These should be checked one by one in class, with the class correcting any wrong answers. In the event of general disagreement over the correct answer, the teacher may ask one student to check the reading text again for the exact answer, while the rest of the class goes on to the next question. When the student has found the sentence or sentences that contain the correct answer, the class may return to that question while the student reads out the pertinent portion of the text to his classmates.

The second exercise provides the student with the opportunity to deal with the main ideas of the reading selections in his own words, by answering questions that require free responses. The teacher may also find these questions useful to assign for composition, with a class that has already had some directed practice in writing English sentences and short paragraphs.

The third exercise requires the student to recognize synonyms for an italic word or italic words in sentences taken from the reading text, or slightly adapted. The correct synonym has to be chosen from among four possible choices for each sentence. This exercise may be done in class or assigned as written homework. The teacher may also ask that, for homework, the student re-write the sentences using the synonyms.

The fourth exercise presents the student with a word study frame based on vocabulary items taken from the reading assignment, and setting out variations of the same items under the headings of adjective, noun, verb and adverb. Following the frame are illustrative sentences using each of the forms found in the chart. This is an extremely valuable exercise for the student, not only because it expands his useable vocabulary, but because it gives him a feeling for the way the different forms fit and "work" in English sentences. The teacher should read the words and illustrative sentences in class, and have individual students point out the form of the word in each sentence and what function it serves.

At the end of the fourth exercise, the student is checked on his ability to use the correct form of the words studied in the word chart and illustrative sentences. This may be done in class, or assigned as written homework, once the teacher has worked through the word chart and illustrative sentences with the students in class.

The authors of this collection have used these short stories and the exercises in their own classes at the University of Isfahan for several years with gratifying success. The stories are always popular with students as well as with teachers.

Isfahan   Robert M. Stevenson
September 1975   Jane L. Stevenson

Stephen Crane

STEPHEN CRANE was born in 1871 and grew up near New York City. He was 24 years old when he wrote his famous novel about the American Civil War, *The Red Badge of Courage*. He had never seen war, but he wrote one of the most powerful war stories in world literature.

After this popular success, Crane sailed on a small ship to Cuba to report on a political revolt, but the ship sank. Out of this experience came his great short story, "The Open Boat."

In this collection are "The Bride Comes to Yellow Sky" and "The Blue Hotel". These are concerned with the inner workings of people and human events. They come alive through the author's unequalled ability to tell a tale.

Crane's style is great because it is simple. The author uncovers emotions that are familiar to everyone, and makes them command the sympathy and understanding of the reader.

Crane's quality of reality set the pace for twentieth century literature. Stephen Crane died in England in 1900, at the age of 29.

The Bride Comes to Yellow Sky
by *Stephen Crane*

The great train was rushing forward with such steady dignity of motion that a glance from the window seemed simply to prove that the flat-lands of Texas were pouring toward the east.

A newly married pair had come on the train at San Antonio. The man's face was reddened from many days in the wind and sun. His roughened hands were continually moving over his new black clothes in a most nervous manner. From time to time he looked down respectfully at his suit. He sat with a hand on each knee, like a man waiting in a shop for a hair-cut. The glances he gave to other passengers were few and quick.

The bride was not pretty, nor was she very young. She wore a dress of blue with many buttons. She continually turned her head to regard some part or other of her dress. It made her feel strange. One could tell that she had cooked and that she expected to cook, dutifully. The searching glances of some of the passengers as she had entered the car had brought the blood rushing to her face. Her uncomfortable expression was strange to see upon this plain face, which was usually calm and almost emotionless.

They were evidently very happy. "Ever been in a train like this before?" he asked, smiling with delight.

"No," she answered, "I never was. It's fine, isn't it?"

"Great! After a while we'll go forward to the dining car and get a big dinner. Finest meal in the world. Costs a dollar."

"Oh, it does?" cried the bride. "A dollar? Oh, that's too much — for us — isn't it, Jack?"

"Not on this trip, at least," he answered bravely. "We're

going to enjoy ourselves."

Later he explained to her about the trains.

"You see, it's a thousand miles from one end of Texas to the other. The train runs straight across it, and only stops four times." He had the pride of an owner. He pointed out to her the beauty of the car they were riding in. And in truth her eyes opened wider as she observed the rich sea-green cloth covering the seats, the shining silver and glass, the wood that shone darkly like the surface of a pool of oil.

To the minds of the pair, their surroundings repeated the glory of their wedding that morning in San Antonio. This was the spirit of their new life, and the man's face in particular shone with a joy that made him appear foolish to certain passengers. In the minds of some, there was supposed to be something hugely funny in the pair's situation.

"We are due at Yellow Sky at 3.42," he said, looking tenderly into her eyes.

"Oh, are we?" she said, as if she had not been aware of it. To show surprise at her husband's remark was part of her wifely duty. She took from a pocket a little silver watch. As she held it before her, and stared at it with a look of attention, the new husband's face shone.

"I bought it in San Antonio from a friend of mine," he told her proudly.

"It's seventeen minutes past twelve," she said, looking up at him with a happy expression which, nevertheless, showed a lack of experience in conversing with men. A passenger, observing her small nervousness, laughed to himself.

At last they went to the dining car. The man serving their table happened to take pleasure in directing them through their meal. He viewed them with the manner of a fatherly guide, his face shining with kindness. But they did not understand his attentions. As they returned to their seats, they showed in their faces a sense of escape.

It was evident that, as the distance from Yellow Sky grew shorter, the husband became nervous. His red hands were even more noticeable. He was rather absent-minded and faraway when the bride leaned forward and spoke to him.

As a matter of truth, Jack Potter was beginning to find his deed weighing upon him like a great stone. He, the town policeman of Yellow Sky, was a man known, liked, and feared in his community. He — an important person — had gone to San Antonio to meet a girl he believed he loved. And there he had actually married her without discussing any part of the matter with Yellow Sky. He was now bringing his bride to a sure-to-be-surprised town.

Of course, people in Yellow Sky married as it pleased them. But Potter's thoughts of his duty to his friends, or of their idea of his duty, made him feel he was sinful. He was guilty of a great and unusual crime. Face to face with this girl in San Antonio, he had leaped over all the social fences. At San Antonio he was like a man hidden in the dark. A knife to cut any friendly duty was easy to take in his hand in that distant city. But the hour of Yellow Sky — the hour of daylight — was approaching.

He knew very well that his wedding was an important thing to the town. It could only be equalled by the burning of the new hotel. His friends could not forgive him, he felt. And now the train was hurrying him toward a scene of surprise, merriment and blame. He glanced out of the window again.

Yellow Sky had a kind of band, which played its horns and drums painfully, to the delight of the people. He laughed without heart as he thought of it. If the citizens could dream of his arrival with his bride, they would march the band at the station and accompany them, among cheers and laughter, to his house.

He decided that he would use all methods of speed and cleverness in making the journey from the station to his house. Once safely at home, he would announce the news. Then he would not go among the citizens until they had time to master their emotions.

The bride looked anxiously at him. "What's worrying you, Jack?"

He laughed. "I'm not worrying, girl. I'm only thinking of Yellow Sky."

She understood, and her face turned red again.

They shared a sense of slight guilt that developed a finer tenderness. They looked at each other with eyes softly glowing. But Potter often laughed the same nervous laugh; the deep red color upon the bride's face did not lessen.

"We're nearly there," he said.

As the train began to slow, they moved forward in the

car. The long line of cars moved into the station of Yellow Sky.

"The train has to get water here," said Potter, from a tight throat and face, as one announcing death. Before the train stopped, his eye had searched the station, and he was glad and surprised to see there was no one there except the station master.

"Come on, girl," said Potter with a thick voice. As he helped her down, they each laughed in a strained manner. He took her bag and told his wife to hold his arm. As they hurried away he saw that the station master had turned and was running toward them, waving his arms. Potter laughed, and sighed as he laughed, when he realized the first effect of his wedding upon Yellow Sky. He grasped his wife's arm firmly to his side and they hurried away.

The California train was due at Yellow Sky in twenty-one minutes. There were six men in the Weary Gentleman Saloon. One was a salesman who talked a great deal and rapidly; three were Texans who did not care to talk at that time; and two were Mexican sheep farmers who did not usually talk in the saloon. The saloon-keeper's dog lay in front of the door. His head was resting on his feet, and he glanced sleepily here and there with the ready watchfulness of a dog that is sometimes kicked. Across the sandy street were some bright green grass spots, so wonderful in appearance next to burning sands in the hot sun. At the cooler side of the railroad station, a man without a coat sat in a chair leaned back against the building. He smoked his pipe. The waters of the Rio Grande river circled near the town, and beyond it could be seen great flatlands.

Except for the busy salesman and his companions in the saloon, Yellow Sky was sleeping. The salesman leaned easily upon a table and told many tales with the confidence of a story teller who had found new listeners.

He was interrupted by a young man who suddenly appeared in the open door. He cried, "Scratchy Wilson's drunk, and has started to make trouble." The two Mexicans at once put down their glasses and disappeared through the rear door of the saloon.

The salesman, not understanding the importance of the warning, jokingly answered, "All right, old man. Suppose he has? Come in and have a drink anyhow."

But the information had made such an apparent impression on everyone in the room that the salesman was forced to see its importance. All had become instantly serious. "Well," he said, filled with mystery, "what is this?" His three companions started to tell him, but the young man at the door stopped them.

"It means, my friend," he answered as he came into the saloon, "that for the next two hours this town won't be very healthy."

The saloon-keeper went to the door and locked it. Reaching out of the window, he pulled in heavy wooden boards which covered the windows, and locked them. The salesman was looking from one to another.

"What is this, anyhow?" he cried. "You don't mean there is going to be a gun-fight?"

"Don't know whether there will be a fight or not," answered one man firmly, "but there'll be some shooting — some good shooting."

The young man who had warned them waved his hand. "Oh, there'll be a fight fast enough, if anyone wanted it. Anybody can get a fight out there in the street. There's a fight just waiting."

The salesman seemed to be realizing the possibility of personal danger.

"What did you say his name was?" he asked.

"Scratchy Wilson," voices answered together.

"And will he kill anybody? What are you going to do? Does this happen often? Can he break in that door?"

"No, he can't break in that door," replied the saloon-keeper. "He's tried it three times. But when he comes, you'd better lie down on the floor, stranger. He's sure to shoot at the door, and a bullet may come through."

After that, the salesman watched the door steadily. The time had not yet come for him to drop to the floor, but he carefully moved near the wall. "Will he kill anybody?" he asked again.

The men laughed, without humor, at the question.

"He's here to shoot, and he's here for trouble. I don't see any good in experimenting with him."

"But what do you do in a situation like this? What do you do?"

A man answered, "Well, he and Jack Potter — "

"But," the other men interrupted together, "Jack Potter's in San Antonio."

"Well, who is he? What's he got to do with this?"

"Oh, he's the town policeman. He goes out and fights Scratchy when he starts acting this way."

A nervous, waiting silence was upon them. The salesman saw that the saloon-keeper, without a sound, had taken a gun from a hiding place. Then he saw a man signal to him, so he moved across the room.

"You'd better come with me behind this table."

"No, thanks," said the salesman. "I'd rather be where I can get out the back door."

At that, the saloon-keeper made a kindly but forceful motion. The salesman obeyed, and found himself seated on a box with his head below the level of the table. The saloon-keeper sat comfortably upon a box nearby.

"You see," he answered, "Scratchy Wilson is a wonder with a gun — a perfect wonder. And when he gets excited, everyone gets out of his path. He's a terror when he's drunk. When he's not drinking he's all right — wouldn't hurt anything — nicest fellow in town. But when he's drunk — be careful!"

There were periods of stillness. "I wish Jack Potter were back from San Antonio," said the saloon-keeper. "He shot Wilson once — in the leg. He'd come in and take care of this thing."

Soon they heard from a distance the sound of a shot, followed by three wild screams. The men looked at each other. "Here he comes," they said.

A man in a red shirt turned a corner and walked into the middle of the main street of Yellow Sky. In each hand the man held a long, heavy, blue-black gun. Often he screamed, and these cries rang through a seemingly deserted village. The screams sounded sharply over the roofs with a power that seemed to have no relation to the ordinary strength of a man's voice. These fierce cries rang against walls of silence.

The man's face flamed in a hot anger born of whiskey. His eyes, rolling but watchful, hunted the still doorways and windows. He walked with the movement of a midnight cat. As the thoughts came to him, he roared threatening information.

The long guns hung from his hands like feathers; they moved with electric speed. The muscles of his neck straightened and sank, straightened and sank, as passion moved him. The only sounds were his terrible invitations to battle. The calm houses preserved their dignity at the passing of this small thing in the middle of the street.

There was no offer of fight — no offer of fight. The man called to the sky. There were no answers. He screamed and shouted and waved his guns here and everywhere.

Finally the man was at the closed door of the saloon. He went to it, and beating upon it with his gun, demanded a drink.

The door remained closed. He picked up a bit of paper from the street and nailed it to the frame of the door with a knife. He then turned his back upon this place and walked to the opposite side of the street. Turning quickly and easily, he fired the guns at the bit of paper. He missed it by a half-inch. He cursed himself, and went away. Later he comfortably shot out all the windows of the house of his best friend. Scratchy was playing with this town. It was a toy for him.

But still there was no offer of fight. The name of Jack Potter, his ancient enemy, entered his mind. He decided that it would be a good thing if he went to Potter's house, and by shooting at it make him come out and fight. He moved in the direction of his desire, singing some sort of war song.

When he arrived at it, Potter's house presented the same still front as had the other homes. Taking a good position, the man screamed an invitation to battle. But this house regarded him as a great, stone god might have done. It gave no sign. After a little wait, the man screamed more invitations, mixing with them wonderful curses.

After a while came the sight of a man working himself into deepest anger over the stillness of a house. He screamed at it. He shot again and again. He paused only for breath or to reload his guns.

Potter and his bride walked rapidly. sometimes they laughed together, quietly and a little foolishly.

"Next corner, dear," he said finally.

They put forth the efforts of a pair walking against a strong wind.

Potter was ready to point out the first appearance of the

new home. Then, as they turned the corner, they came face to face with the man in the red shirt, who was feverishly loading a large gun. Immediately the man dropped his empty gun to the ground and, like lightning, pulled out another. The second gun was aimed at Potter's chest.

There was a silence. Potter couldn't open his mouth. Quickly he loosened his arm from the woman's grasp, and dropped the bag to the sand. As for the bride, her face had become the color of an old cloth. She was motionless.

The two men faced each other at a distance of nine feet. Behind the gun, Wilson smiled with a new and quiet cruelty.

"Tried to surprise me," he said. "Tried to surprise me!" His eyes grew more evil.

As Potter made a slight movement, the man pushed his gun sharply forward. "No, don't you do it, Jack Potter. Don't you move a finger toward a gun yet. Don't you move a muscle. The time has come for me to settle with you, and I'm going to do it my own way — slowly, with no interruption. So just listen to what I tell you."

Potter looked at his enemy. "I haven't got a gun with me, Scratchy," he said. "Honest, I haven't." He was stiffening and steadying, but at the back of his mind floated a picture of the beautiful car on the train. He thought of the glory of the wedding, the spirit of his new life. "You know I fight when I have to fight, Scratchy Wilson. But I haven't a gun with me. You'll have to do all the shooting yourself."

His enemy's face turned pale with anger. He stepped forward and whipped his gun back and forth before Potter's chest. "Don't tell me a lie like that. There isn't a man in Texas who ever saw you without a gun. Don't think I'm a kid." His eyes burned with anger and his breath came heavily.

"I don't think you're a kid," answered Potter. His feet had not moved an inch backward. "I think you're a complete fool. I tell you I haven't got a gun, and I haven't. If you're going to shoot me, you'd better begin now; you'll never get a chance like this again."

So much enforced reasoning had weakened Wilson's anger; he was calmer. "If you haven't got a gun, why haven't you got a gun?" he asked. "Been to church?"

"I haven't got a gun because I've just come from San Antonio with my wife. I'm married," said Potter. "And if I had thought there'd be a fool like you here when I brought my wife home, I would have had a gun, and don't you forget it."

"Married!" said Scratchy, not at all understanding.

"Yes, married. I'm married," said Potter, clearly.

"Married?" said Scratchy. Seemingly for the first time, he saw the pale, frightened woman at the other man's side. "No!" he said. He was like a creature allowed a glance at another world. He moved a pace backward, and his arm, with the gun, dropped to his side. "Is this the lady?" he asked.

"Yes; this is the lady," answered Potter.

There was another period of silence.

"Well," said Wilson at last, slowly. "I suppose we won't fight now."

"We won't if you say so Scratchy. You know I didn't make the trouble." Potter lifted the bag.

"Well, I guess we won't fight, Jack," said Wilson. He was looking at the ground. "Married!" He was not a student of good manners; it was merely that in the presence of this foreign condition he was a simple child of the wildlands. He picked up his fallen gun, and he went away. His feet made deep tracks in the heavy sand.

COMPREHENSION QUESTIONS

EXERCISE 1 For each question, write down the letter that corresponds to the correct answer. Choose only one.

1 In which direction was the train going that carried the newly married pair?
(a) Towards San Antonio in Texas.
(b) Towards the east.
(c) Towards the west.
(d) The story doesn't say.

2 Which of the following does not describe the bride?
(a) She wasn't pretty.
(b) She was quite old.
(c) She was accustomed to working in kitchens.
(d) She wore a blue dress.

3 Why was it unusual to see an uncomfortable expression

and blush on her face?
(a) Because she was used to having people glance at her.
(b) Because she was usually smiling and looked joyful.
(c) Because she always seemed to be comfortable everywhere.
(d) Because her face was usually without emotion and calm.

4 In describing the beauties of the train to his wife, how did Jack act?
(a) Like a person who didn't believe his own words.
(b) Like the owner of the train.
(c) Like a person who was afraid that his wife didn't realize how lucky she was.
(d) Like a person who exaggerates everything.

5 How did the other passengers react to the married couple?
(a) They paid no attention to them.
(b) They tried to talk to them and be friendly.
(c) They laughed secretly.
(d) They were unkind and considered the couple to be stupid.

6 What was weighing Jack down with worry?
(a) Whether his new wife would like Yellow Sky.
(b) Whether he really loved his new wife.
(c) The fact that he had not discussed his marriage with his community.
(d) The fact that he had been away from his police duty for several days.

7 How important would his marriage be to Yellow Sky?
(a) More important than the burning of the new hotel.
(b) He wasn't yet sure.
(c) The most important event in the history of the town.
(d) As important as the burning of the new hotel would be.

8 When the train arrived in Yellow Sky, how did Jack respond to the station master's greeting?
(a) He ignored it and left the station quickly.
(b) He grasped the station master firmly by the hand.
(c) He laughed and waved his arms at the station master.
(d) He ran towards the station master with his wife.

9 Which of the following was not present in the saloon, as the train approached Yellow Sky?
   (a) Two sheep farmers.
   (b) A salesman.
   (c) A coatless man smoking a pipe.
   (d) Three silent Texans.

10 When a young man appeared suddenly and announced that Scratchy Wilson was drunk and had started to make trouble, what happened immediately?
   (a) The salesman invited the young man in for a drink.
   (b) The three Texans disappeared at once.
   (c) The salesman leaned upon a table and began a story.
   (d) The Mexicans left the saloon.

11 How did the saloon-keeper know that Wilson couldn't break in the saloon door?
   (a) Because he was not a very strong man.
   (b) Because the heavy boards covered the door.
   (c) Because he had tried unsuccessfully before.
   (d) Because the saloon-keeper intended to shoot Wilson first.

12 What kind of a person was Scratchy?
   (a) A natural killer.
   (b) Gentle when sober, but a terror when drunk.
   (c) Without humor.
   (d) Nervous and excitable.

13 Why did the saloon-keeper wish that Jack Potter was there?
   (a) To shoot Scratchy in the leg.
   (b) To kill Scratchy.
   (c) To take care of the problem in the street.
   (d) To provide some excitement for the town.

14 How did the men in the bar know that Scratchy was approaching the saloon?
   (a) From his screams and the shooting of his gun.
   (b) They could see him through a crack in the door.
   (c) He announced his name loudly from the street.
   (d) They could hear his footsteps in the street.

15 What did Scratchy do with his guns as he screamed and shouted invitations to fight?

   (a) He fired them off in every direction.
   (b) He held them straight down on either side of his body.
   (c) He waved them in all directions.
   (d) He changed them from hand to hand.

16 When Jack Potter's house would not answer Scratchy's invitations to fight, what did he do?
   (a) He left and shot out all the windows in a friend's house.
   (b) He screamed and shot at the house again and again.
   (c) He shot holes in the front door of the house.
   (d) He became still and rested for half an hour.

17 When the couple met Scratchy at the corner, what did Scratchy do?
   (a) He loaded both guns and pointed them at the couple.
   (b) He fired both guns into the air.
   (c) He dropped the empty gun and pointed the other at Jack.
   (d) He fired one gun so that the bullet almost struck Jack.

18 As Jack tried to convince Scratchy that he didn't have a gun, what thoughts were in his mind?
   (a) Of the damage to his house and property.
   (b) Of his life as a married man.
   (c) Of his wife's future if he were to die.
   (d) Of his strong desire to kill Scratchy.

19 Why did Scratchy refuse to believe that Potter didn't have a gun?
   (a) Because he thought Potter had one in the bag.
   (b) Because in his drunkenness he thought he could see a gun in Potter's right hand.
   (c) Because he thought he could see a gun in Potter's back pocket.
   (d) Because no Texan had ever seen the policeman without a gun.

20 Why did Scratchy first think that Potter might not have a gun?
   (a) Because he had stopped fighting.
   (b) Because he had been to church.
   (c) Because he had lost it.
   (d) Because his new wife had taken it away from him.

21 How did Scratchy react to Potter's announcement that he was married?
  (a) He refused to believe it.
  (b) He thought it was funny.
  (c) He grew ashamed of himself.
  (d) At first he didn't understand.

22 Why did Scratchy say, "I suppose we won't fight now?"
  (a) Because he did not want to shoot in the presence of a woman.
  (b) Because conditions had changed and were no longer right for fighting.
  (c) Because he really had good manners.
  (d) Because Potter didn't have a gun.

QUESTIONS FOR DISCUSSION AND WRITING PRACTICE

EXERCISE 2 The following questions may be used for classroom discussion, for written homework, or for both.

1 Describe the two individuals who have just been married. What work had these two people done before marriage?

2 Why did Potter feel "sinful" about not giving advance notice of his marriage to the people of Yellow Sky? In what way was he different from other citizens?

3 What happened in Yellow Sky when Scratchy got drunk and went into the streets with his guns?

4 Describe the precautions which the saloon-keeper took when he heard that Scratchy was drunk and angry.

5 Describe the newly married couple's movements from the time they arrived in Yellow Sky until they met Scratchy.

6 Why was Potter's constant presence in Yellow Sky so important?

7 What made Scratchy decide not to fight Potter?

8 Is there anyone like Jack Potter in your community? Is your community at all like Yellow Sky?

SYNONYMS

EXERCISE 3 For each question, write down the letter that corresponds to the correct synonym for the word(s) in italics.

1 Potter's *roughened* hands were continually moving over his new black clothes in a most nervous manner.
(a) ugly (b) rude (c) toughened (d) reddened

2 The *searching* glances of some of the passengers as she had entered the car had brought the blood rushing to her face.
(a) analysis (b) penetrating (c) looking (d) investigation

3 Her uncomfortable expression was strange to see upon this *plain* face, which was usually calm and almost emotionless.
(a) flat (b) clear (c) empty (d) homely

4 Face to face with this girl in San Antonio, Potter had *leaped over* all the social fences.
(a) climbed (b) broken (c) hurried (d) by-passed

5 If the citizens could dream of Potter's arrival with his bride, they would march the band at the station and *accompany* them, among cheers and laughter, to his house.
(a) help (b) carry (c) escort (d) invite

6 As Potter helped his wife down from the train, they both laughed in a *strained* manner.
(a) filtered (b) stretched (c) tense (d) pulled

7 The dog glanced sleepily here and there with the ready *watchfulness* of a dog that is sometimes kicked.
(a) suspicion (b) wakefulness (c) worry (d) vigilance

8 Scratchy's cries rang through a seemingly *deserted* village.
(a) sandy (b) wilderness (c) worthy (d) forsaken

9 The calm houses *preserved* their dignity at the passing of this small thing in the middle of the street.
(a) saved (b) presented (c) maintained (d) took care of

10 The second gun was *aimed* at Potter's chest.
(a) pointed (b) intended (c) target (d) direction

WORD STUDY

EXERCISE 4 Study these words and the sentences that follow them. If possible, repeat them after your teacher. The word in italics in the table is the form found in your reading.

WORD CHART

	ADJECTIVE	NOUN	VERB	ADVERB
1	married, unmarried, marriageable	marriage	*marry*	
2	emotional, unemotional, emotionless	*emotion*		emotionally, unemotionally
3	*forceful,* forced	force	force, enforce	forcefully
4	*threatening,* threatened	threat	threaten	threateningly
5	loaded, unloaded	load	*load,* reload, unload	

1 People in Yellow Sky *married* as it pleased them. Their *marriages* were personal arrangements not based on the wishes of family or friends. Most people in Yellow Sky got *married*. There were very few *unmarried* adult citizens. The *married* people outnumbered the *unmarried* ones. Very few citizens of either sex in Yellow Sky were not *marriageable*.

2 Potter decided not to go among the citizens until they had time to master their *emotions*. Because they liked Potter, they were sure to have an *emotional* reaction to the news that he was married. Very few of his friends could remain *unemotional* about such news. If they knew he was arriving with his bride, they would certainly greet him *emotionally* at the railroad station. Only those citizens who didn't know Potter well could receive the good news *unemotionally*.

Potter's bride had had an almost *emotionless* face before he met her, but now her *emotion* for her husband showed clearly.

3 The saloon-keeper made a kindly but *forceful* motion to the salesman. If necessary, he would have *forced* the salesman to sit behind the table. There was *force* in the saloon-keeper's personality as well as in his muscles. He spoke *forcefully* although politely to the salesman. As saloon-keeper he *enforced* the rules of the saloon.

4 As the thoughts came to Scratchy in the streets, he roared *threatening* information. The *threatened* citizens stayed behind their locked doors. Scratchy's *threats* emptied the streets of all peace-loving citizens. He *threatened* them with murder and destruction. He roared *threateningly* at all the quiet houses.

5 Scratchy was feverishly *loading* a large gun as the couple came around the corner. Immediately the man dropped his *unloaded* gun to the ground and pulled out a *loaded* one. As soon as a gun was empty, he *reloaded* it. He *unloaded* each gun by firing it at the quiet house. With the *load* in each gun, he was able to break many windows and cause a lot of damage.

Complete each sentence with the correct form of the word given before each sentence. The word given is the form found in your reading. Refer to the word chart if necessary.

1 *marry*   Most men remain _____ until they are able to support a family.
In western countries, _____ is losing its attractions for many women.

2 *emotions* In Anglo-Saxon countries, male children are raised to remain _____ even in the face of great grief or joy.
The birth of a child is an _____ occasion for most parents.

3 *forceful* Education is not something which can be accomplished by _____.

No government can _____ an unreasonable law for very long.

4 *threaten-* Polluted air _____ the health of people
   ing   in most large cities.

People who smoke tobacco heavily face a
_____ of lung cancer and heart trouble.

5 *load*   Many accidental deaths have occurred because a
careless person left a _____ gun near in-
nocent people.

Before automatic weapons were developed, it was
necessary to _____ a gun each time it was
fired.

The Blue Hotel
by Stephen Crane

The Palace Hotel at Fort Romper was painted a light blue, a color of blue found on the legs of a certain bird that makes it bright in any surroundings. The Palace Hotel, then, looked always loud and screaming in a way that made the bright winter scenes of Nebraska seem only a dull gray. It stood alone, and when the snow was falling, the town two hundred yards away could not be seen.

When a traveler came from the railroad station, he was obliged to pass the Palace Hotel before he came to the group of low houses which was Fort Romper. It was believed that no traveler could pass the Palace Hotel without looking at it. Pat Scully, the hotel-owner, had proved himself a master at choosing paints. It is true that on clear days, when the long lines of trains swept through Fort Romper, passengers were surprised at the sight. Those that knew of the brown-reds and the dark greens of the eastern part of the country laughingly expressed shame, pity, shock. But to the citizens of this western town and to the people who stopped there, Pat Scully had performed a wonder.

As if the displayed delights of such a blue hotel were not sufficiently inviting, Scully went every morning and evening to meet the trains that stopped at Romper. He would express greetings and welcome to anyone he might see hesitating.

One morning when a snow-covered engine dragged its long string of cars to the station, Scully performed the marvelous trick of catching three men. One was a shaky and quick-eyed Swede, with a great, shining, cheap bag; one was a tall, sun-browned cowboy, who was on his way to a job near the Dakota border; one was a little silent man from the east coast, who didn't look like it and didn't announce it.

Scully practically made them prisoners. He was so quick and merry and kindly that each probably felt it would be cruel to try to escape. So they followed the eager little man. He wore a heavy fur cap pulled tightly down on his head. It caused his two red ears to stand out stiffly, as if they were made of tin.

At last, Scully grandly conducted them through the door of the blue hotel. The room which they entered was small. It was occupied mostly by a huge stove in the center, which was burning with great force. At various points on its surface the iron had become shiny and glowed yellow from the heat. Beside the stove, Scully's son, Johnnie, was playing a game of cards with an old farmer. They were quarreling.

With loud words Scully stopped their play, and hurried his son upstairs with the bags of the new guests. He himself led them to three bowls of icy water. The cowboy and the Easterner washed themselves in this water until they were as red as fire. The Swede, however, merely placed his fingers in the bowl. It was noticeable throughout these proceedings that the three travelers were made to feel that Scully was very kind indeed. He was giving out great favors.

Afterward they returned to the first room. There, sitting about the stove, they listened to Scully shouting at his daughters, who were preparing the noon meal. They employed the silence of experienced men who move carefully among new people. The Swede was especially silent. He seemed to be occupied in making secret judgments of each man in the room. One might have thought that he had the sense of foolish fear which accompanies guilt. He looked like a badly frightened man.

Later, at dinner, he spoke little, directing his conversation entirely to Scully. He said that he had come from New York, where he had worked for ten years as a suitmaker. These facts seemed to interest Scully, and afterward he told them that he had lived at Romper for fourteen years. The Swede asked about the crops and the price of labor. He seemed hardly to listen to Scully's lengthy replies. His eyes continued to wander from man to man.

Finally, with a laugh, he said that some of these Western towns were very dangerous; and after this declaration he straightened his legs under the table, nodded his head, and laughed again, loudly. It was plain that this had no meaning to the others. They looked at him, wondering and in silence.

After dinner, it was decided to play a game of cards. The cowboy offered to play with Johnnie, and they all turned to ask the Swede to play with the little Easterner. The Swede asked some questions about the game. Learning that it wore many names, and that he had played it under another name, he accepted the invitation.

He came toward the men nervously, as though he expected to be attacked. Finally, seated, he looked from face to face and laughed sharply. This laugh was so strange that the Easterner looked up quickly, the cowboy sat with his mouth open, and Johnnie paused, holding the cards with still fingers.

Afterward there was a short silence. Then Johnnie said, "Well, let's begin. Come on now!" They pulled their chairs forward until their knees touched under the table. They began to play, and their interest in the game caused the others to forget the strange ways of the Swede.

Suddenly the Swede spoke to Johnnie: "I suppose there have been a good many men killed in this room." The mouths of the others dropped open and they looked at him.

"What are you talking about?" said Johnnie.

The Swede laughed again his loud laugh, full of a kind of false courage. "Oh, you know what I mean all right," he answered.

"I don't!" Johnnie protested. The card game stopped, and the men stared at the Swede. Johnnie evidently felt that as the son of the hotel-owner he should make a direct inquiry. "Now, what are you trying to say?" he asked.

The Swede's fingers shook on the edge of the table. "Oh, maybe you think I haven't been anywhere. Maybe you think I don't have any experience?"

"I don't know anything about you," answered Johnnie, "and I don't care where you've been. I just don't know what you're trying to say. Nobody has ever been killed in this room."

The cowboy, who had been steadily gazing at the Swede, then spoke: "What's wrong with you, fellow?"

Apparently it seemed to the Swede that he was powerfully threatened. He trembled, and turned pale near the corners of his mouth. He sent an appealing glance in the direction of the little Easterner. "They say they don't know what I mean," he remarked bitterly to the Easterner.

The latter answered after long and careful thought. "I don't understand you," he said calmly.

The Swede made a movement then which announced that he thought he had met attack from the only place where he had expected sympathy, if not help. "I see that you're all against me. I see—"

The cowboy felt as though he had lost his senses. "Say," he cried, as he threw the cards fiercely down upon the table, "say, what are you trying to do?"

The Swede jumped up. "I don't want to fight!" he shouted. "I don't want to fight!"

The cowboy stretched his long legs slowly and carefully. His hands were in his pockets. "Well, who thought you did?" he inquired.

The Swede moved rapidly back toward a corner of the room. His hands were out protectingly in front of his chest, but he was making an apparent struggle to control his fright. "Gentlemen," he almost whispered, "I suppose I am going to be killed before I can leave this house! I suppose I am going to be killed before I can leave this house!"

A door opened, and Scully himself entered. He paused in surprise as he noted the terror-filled eyes of the Swede. Then he said, "What's the matter here?"

The Swede answered him quickly and eagerly: "These men are going to kill me."

"Kill you!" shouted Scully. "Kill you! What are you talking about?"

The Swede put out his hands helplessly.

Scully turned upon his son. "What is this, Johnnie?"

The lad had become ill-tempered. "I don't know," he answered. "It doesn't make any sense to me." He began to pick up the cards, gathering them together angrily. "He says a good many men have been killed in this room, or something like that. And he says he's going to be killed here, too. I don't know what's wrong with him. He's probably crazy."

Scully then looked for explanation to the cowboy, but the cowboy simply shook his head.

"Kill you?" said Scully again to the Swede. "Kill you? Man, you're crazy."

"Oh, I know," burst out the Swede. "I know what will happen. Yes, I'm crazy — yes. Yes, of course, I'm crazy — yes. But I know one thing—" There was suffering and terror upon his face. "I know I won't get out of here alive."

Scully turned and faced his son. "You've been troubling this man!"

Johnnie's voice was loud with its burden of undeserved blame. "Why, good God, I haven't done anything to him!"

The Swede broke in. "Gentlemen, do not trouble yourselves. I will leave this house. I will go away, because—" he blamed them with his glance — "because I do not want to be killed."

"You will not go away," said Scully. "You will not go away until I hear the reason of this business. If anybody has troubled you, I will take care of him. This is my house. You are under my roof, and I will not allow any peaceful man to be troubled here." He looked threateningly at Johnnie, the cowboy and the Easterner.

"Don't, Mr Scully, don't. I will go away. I do not wish to be killed." The Swede moved toward the door which opened to the stairs. It was evidently his intention to go at once for his bag.

"No, no," shouted Scully commandingly; but the pale-faced man slipped by him and disappeared. "Now," said Scully angrily to the others, "what does this mean?"

Johnnie and the cowboy cried together: "Why, we didn't do anything to him!"

Scully's eyes were cold. "No," he said, "you didn't?"

Johnnie repeated his words. "Why, this is the wildest madman I ever saw. We didn't do anything at all. We were just sitting here playing cards, and he—"

The father suddenly spoke to the Easterner. "What have these boys been doing?"

The Easterner thought again. "I didn't see anything wrong at all," he said at last, slowly.

Scully began to shout. "But what does it mean?" He stared fiercely at his son. "I ought to beat you for this, my boy."

Johnnie was wild. "Well, what have I done?" he screamed at his father.

"I think you are tongue-tied," said Scully finally to his

son, the cowboy and the Easterner; and at the end of this
sentence he left the room.

Upstairs the Swede was closing his bag. His back was half-
turned toward the door, and hearing a noise there, he turned
and jumped up, uttering a loud cry. Scully's face was
frightening in the light of the small lamp he carried. This
yellow shine, streaming upward, left his eyes in deep shadows.
He looked like a murderer.

"Man! Man!" exclaimed Scully. "Have you gone mad?"

"Oh, no! Oh, no!" answered the other. "There are people
in this world who know nearly as much as you do —
understand?"

For a moment they stood gazing at each other. Then
Scully placed the light on the table and sat himself on the edge
of the bed. He spoke slowly. "I never heard of such a thing in
my life. It's a complete mystery. I can't think how you ever got
this idea into your head." Then Scully lifted his eyes and
asked, "And did you really think that they were going to kill
you?"

The Swede looked at the old man as if he wished to see
into his mind. "I did," he said at last. He apparently thought
that his answer might cause an attack. As he worked on his
bag his whole arm shook, the elbow trembling like a bit of
paper.

Having finished his bag, the Swede straightened himself.
"Mr Scully," he said with sudden courage, "how much do I
owe you?"

"You don't owe me anything," said the old man angrily.

"Yes, I do," answered the Swede. He took some money
from his pocket and held it out to Scully, but the latter moved
his hand away in firm refusal.

"I won't take your money," said Scully. "Not after what's
been happening here." Then a plan seemed to come to him.
"Here," he cried, picking up his lamp and moving toward the
door. "Here! Come with me a minute."

"No," said the Swede in great alarm.

"Yes," urged the old man. "Come on! I want you to come
— just across the hall — in my room."

The Swede must have decided that the hour of his death
had come. His mouth dropped open and his teeth showed like
a dead man's. He at last followed Scully across the hall, but he

had the step of one hung in chains.

"Now," said the old man. He dropped suddenly to the floor and put his head beneath the bed. The Swede could hear his dulled voice. "I'd keep it under my pillow if it weren't for that boy Johnnie. Where is it now? I never put it twice in the same place. There — now, come out!"

Finally, he came out from under the bed, dragging with him an old coat. "I've got it," he whispered. Still on the floor on his knees, he unrolled the coat and took from it a large, yellow-brown whiskey bottle.

His first act was to hold the bottle up to the light. Satisfied, apparently, that nobody had touched it, he pushed it with a generous movement toward the Swede.

The weak-kneed Swede was about to eagerly grasp this element of strength, but suddenly he pulled his hand away and cast a look of horror upon Scully.

"Drink," said the old man in a friendly tone. He had risen to his feet, and now stood facing the Swede.

There was a silence. Then again Scully said, "Drink!"

The Swede laughed wildly. He seized the bottle, put it to his mouth. And as his lips curled foolishly around the opening, and his throat worked, he kept his glance, burning with hate, upon the old man's face.

After the departure of Scully, the three men, still at the table, sat for a long moment in surprised silence. Then Johnnie said, "That's the worst man I ever saw."

"Oh, I don't know," replied the Easterner.

"Well, what do you think makes him act that way?" asked the cowboy.

"He's frightened." The Easterner knocked his pipe against the stove. "He's frightened right out of his senses."

"At what?" asked Johnnie and the cowboy together.

"I don't know, but it seems to me this man has been reading cheap novels about the West, and he think's he's right in the middle of it — the shooting and killing and all."

"But," said the cowboy, deeply shocked, "this isn't a wild place. This is Nebraska."

"Yes," added Johnnie, "and why doesn't he wait until he really gets out West?"

The traveled Easterner laughed. "Things aren't bad even there — not in these days. But he thinks he's right in the middle of hell."

Johnnie and the cowboy thought for a long while.

"It's strange," remarked Johnnie at last.

"Yes," said the cowboy. "This is a queer game. I hope we don't get a lot of snow, because then we'd have this man with us all of the time. That wouldn't be any good."

Soon they heard a loud voice on the stairs, accompanied by jokes in the voice of old Scully; and laughter, evidently from the Swede. The men around the stove stared in surprise at each other. The door swung open, and Scully and the Swede came into the room.

Five chairs were now placed in a circle about the stove. The Swede began to talk, loudly and angrily. Johnnie, the cowboy, and the Easterner remained silent while old Scully appeared to be eager and full of sympathy.

Finally the Swede announced that he wanted a drink of water. He moved his chair, and said he would go and get some.

"I'll get it for you," said Scully at once.

"No," refused the Swede roughly. "I'll get it for myself." He got up and walked with the manner of an owner into another part of the hotel.

As soon as the Swede was out of the room, Scully jumped to his feet and whispered quickly to the others: "Upstairs he thought I was trying to poison him."

"This makes me sick," said Johnnie. "Why don't you throw him out in the snow?"

"He's all right now," declared Scully. "He was from the East, and he thought this was a rough place. That's all. He's all right now."

The cowboy looked with admiration upon the Easterner. "You were right," he said.

"Well," said Johnnie to his father, "he may be all right now, but I don't understand it. Before, he was afraid, but now he's too brave."

Scully now spoke to his son. "What do I keep? What do I keep? What do I keep?" he demanded in a voice like thunder. He struck his knee sharply to indicate that he himself was going to make reply, and that all should listen. "I keep a hotel," he shouted. "A hotel, do you hear? A guest under my roof has special privileges. He is not to be threatened. Not one

word shall he hear that would make him want to go away.
There's no place in this town where they can say they took in a
guest of mine because he was afraid to stay here." He turned
suddenly on the cowboy and the Easterner. "Am I right?"

"Yes, Mr Scully," said the cowboy, "I think you're right."

"Yes, Mr Scully," said the Easterner, "I think you're
right."

(to be continued)

COMPREHENSION QUESTIONS

EXERCISE 1 For each question, write down the letter that
corresponds to the correct answer. Choose only one.

1 What effect did the blueness of the Palace Hotel have on
the winter scenes of Nebraska?
(a) It made them all seem two hundred yards away.
(b) None of the scenes could be seen.
(c) The winter scenes became a dull gray.
(d) It made the winter scenes loud and screaming.

2 How did Fort Romper citizens and visitors feel about the
blue hotel?
(a) They thought it was wonderful.
(b) They disliked it but they felt they must defend it.
(c) They liked it better than the brown-reds and greens.
(d) They never thought about it at all.

3 One winter morning Pat Scully managed to "catch" some
men at the railroad station. Which of these did he not
catch?
(a) A little Easterner.
(b) A Californian in a heavy fur cap.
(c) A tall cowboy.
(d) A quick-eyed Swede.

4 How did Scully make the guests feel that it would be cruel
to try to escape?
(a) By telling them of his poverty and hardship.
(b) By impressing them with how lonely he was.
(c) By reminding them that they were his prisoners.
(d) By being cheerful and kindly to them.

5 As the new guests sat around the hotel stove for the first
time, how did they regard each other?
   (a) Fearfully.
   (b) Silently.
   (c) Foolishly.
   (d) Guiltily.

6 What behavior of the Swede had no meaning to the other
guests?
   (a) His habit of not listening to other people.
   (b) His loud, sharp laughter.
   (c) The nodding of his head.
   (d) His silence.

7 When the Swede suggested that many men had been killed
in the room where they were playing cards, how did the
other guests react?
   (a) They laughed loudly.
   (b) They shouted at him angrily.
   (c) Their mouths fell open.
   (d) They threw their cards on the floor.

8 How did the Swede receive the denials of killings and the
questions about his own behavior?
   (a) He was half convinced by them.
   (b) He refused to believe them.
   (c) He was reassured and more relaxed.
   (d) He called all of the other guests liars.

9 What did the cowboy do that made the Swede think that he
wanted to fight?
   (a) He threw his cards fiercely down on the table.
   (b) He jumped up and looked the Swede in the face.
   (c) He knocked the card table over.
   (d) He stretched his long legs and put his hands in his
       pockets.

10 How did Johnnie explain the Swede's behavior to his
father?
   (a) He said that the Swede was probably a killer.
   (b) He said that the Swede had been cheating at cards.
   (c) He said that the Swede was probably crazy.
   (d) He said that the Swede was probably drunk.

11 Whom did Scully blame for the Swede's trouble?
(a) His son.
(b) The Swede himself.
(c) All of the guests.
(d) Himself.

12 What reason did Scully give for not allowing the Swede to go away?
(a) He had not yet paid his bill.
(b) As a guest he was under the protection of the hotel-owner.
(c) He must first explain why he thought there had been killings in the hotel.
(d) He must not tell the others bad stories about the Palace Hotel.

13 How did Scully receive the guests' protests that they had done nothing to the Swede?
(a) He was very suspicious.
(b) He believed them but wouldn't admit it.
(c) He refused to listen to their protests.
(d) He disbelieved the guests, but believed his son.

14 Why do you think Scully told the guests that they were "tongue-tied"?
(a) Because he thought all of them were liars.
(b) Because no one was able to explain the Swede's behavior.
(c) Because all of them had agreed to be silent.
(d) Because they wouldn't blame Johnnie for the trouble.

15 When Scully entered the Swede's room, why did he look like a murderer?
(a) Because he had murder in his heart.
(b) Because he wanted to murder his son, Johnnie.
(c) Because the light from a small lamp made him look like a murderer.
(d) Because he felt like murdering the Swede.

16 After the Swede's bag was packed, why did Scully refuse to accept money from him?
(a) Because the Swede had only arrived at the hotel.
(b) Because as a guest he had been treated badly.

(c) Because Scully had grown fond of the Swede.

(d) Because Scully never accepted money any place except the office.

17 How did Scully hide the bottle of whiskey?
 (a) Wrapped in an old coat and hidden under his pillow.
 (b) Wrapped in paper and put under the mattress.
 (c) Wrapped in a coat and put behind the bed.
 (d) Wrapped in an old coat and hidden under the bed.

18 How did the Easterner explain the Swede's behavior to the other guests?
 (a) He said that the Swede drank too much.
 (b) He said that the Swede was perhaps an escaped criminal.
 (c) He said that the Swede was extremely frightened.
 (d) He said that the Swede needed their friendship and help.

19 Why did the Easterner think the Swede held the ideas that he had?
 (a) Because he had perhaps had other bad experiences in the West.
 (b) Because his friends in the East had warned him of the West.
 (c) Because he had read popular books about shootings, killings, etc., in the West.
 (d) Because he had bad ideas about people everywhere.

20 Why did the cowboy hope that they wouldn't "get a lot of snow"?
 (a) Because the Swede could not leave.
 (b) Because then the trains would all be late.
 (c) Because then they would all have to remain inside the hotel.
 (d) Because then the cowboy could not leave for Dakota.

21 Why did the cowboy look with admiration upon the Easterner?
 (a) Because the Easterner was right about the Swede's fear.
 (b) Because the Easterner seemed to be afraid of nothing.
 (c) Because the Easterner suggested throwing the Swede out in the snow.

(d) Because the Easterner had read many books and seemed wise.

22 What change did Johnnie think had come over the Swede?
  (a) He had become even more frightened.
  (b) He had grown very calm and quiet.
  (c) He had become too brave.
  (d) He had become very friendly.

23 What was the most important reason for Scully's efforts to keep the Swede in the hotel?
  (a) There was no other hotel in the town.
  (b) Scully felt a sense of obligation to his guests.
  (c) Scully didn't want anyone in the town to say that a guest left the hotel because of fear.
  (d) Scully needed the money which the Swede owed for his room.

24 Who agreed with Scully?
  (a) The Easterner and the cowboy.
  (b) Everybody.
  (c) Johnnie.
  (d) Nobody.

QUESTIONS FOR DISCUSSION AND WRITING PRACTICE

EXERCISE 2 The following questions may be used for classroom discussion, for written homework, or for both.

1 How did the Palace Hotel contrast with its surroundings?

2 What kind of hotel manager was Pat Scully?

3 Describe the three guests in our story.

4 How did the Swede first disturb the tranquillity of the others?

5 What explanation did the Easterner give for the Swede's behavior?

6 How did Scully try to get the Swede to relax?

7 How would you describe the relationship between Scully and his son?

8 Why was Scully especially anxious that the Swede should not leave the hotel?

9 What do you notice about the way that the Easterner answers any questions that are asked of him? What does this show about him?

10 What evidence is there that the Swede was perhaps a heavy drinker?

SYNONYMS

EXERCISE 3 For each question, write down the letter that corresponds to the correct synonym for the word(s) in italics.

1 The hotel was a color of blue found on the legs of a certain bird that makes it bright in any *surroundings.*
(a) circles (b) boundaries (c) environment (d) neighborhood

2 To the citizens of Fort Romper, Scully had *performed* a wonder.
(a) acted (b) took part in (c) painted (d) achieved

3 Johnnie and an old farmer were playing cards and *quarreling.*
(a) argument (b) cheating (c) debating (d) squabbling

4 The guests *employed* the silence of experienced men who move carefully among new people.
(a) hired (b) engaged (c) used (d) occupied

5 It seemed to the Swede that he was powerfully *threatened.*
(a) endanger (b) menaced (c) challenged (d) injured

6 The Swede sent an *appealing* glance in the direction of the little Easterner.
(a) entreating (b) enchanting (c) attractive (d) humble

7 "You've been *troubling* this man!" said Scully to his son.
(a) difficulty (b) disturbing (c) injuring (d) threatening

8 "This is the wildest *madman* I ever saw," said Johnnie.
(a) angry person (b) devil (c) insane (d) lunatic

9 "I think you are *tongue-tied*," said Scully to his guests.
(a) lying (b) silent with dishonesty (c) unable to speak (d) in agreement to be silent

10 The cowboy looked with *admiration* upon the Easterner.
(a) flattery (b) approbation (c) envy (d) adoration.

WORD STUDY

EXERCISE 4 Study these words and the sentences that follow them. If possible, repeat them after your teacher. The word in italics in the table is the form found in your reading.

WORD CHART

	ADJECTIVE	NOUN	VERB	ADVERB
1	laughing, laughable	laugh, laughter	laugh	*laughingly*
2	*experienced,* inexperienced	experience	experience	
3	judged	judge, *judgment*	judge	
4	guilty, guiltless, guiltridden	*guilt*		guiltily, guiltlessly
5	*dangerous*	danger	endanger	dangerously

1 Train passengers *laughingly* expressed shame, pity, shock at the color of the Palace Hotel. They thought the choice of colors was *laughable.* One could see their *laughing* faces in the windows of the train. While the trains were in Fort Romper station, loud *laughs* came from some of the Eastern passengers. Their *laughter* offended the citizens of Fort Romper. The passengers *laughed* because they thought the hotel was a vulgar color.

2 The guests employed the silence of *experienced* men who move carefully among new people. *Inexperienced* guests might have begun to talk at once. Travelers learn from *experience* to consider their fellow-travelers before beginning a conversation. Those who talk too soon have often *experienced* the boredom of having to listen to a fellow-passenger who never stops talking.

3 At the dinner table, the Swede seemed to be occupied in making secret *judgments* of each man in the room. The *judged* men sat eating in silence. The Swede was their self-appointed *judge*. He *judged* them all severely. He *judged* them to be killers.

4 One might have thought that the Swede had the sense of foolish fear which accompanies *guilt*. He had a *guilty* look about him. When Scully accused his son of troubling the Swede, Johnnie claimed to be completely *guiltless*. He stared *guiltlessly* at his accusing father. Because he felt responsible, Scully glanced *guiltily* at the frightened Swede. He was *guilt-ridden* by the thought that a guest had been mistreated.

5 With a laugh, the Swede said that some of the Western towns were very *dangerous*. He believed that his life was constantly in *danger* in the West. He did not enjoy living *dangerously*. He was sure that he had *endangered* his life by leaving New York.

Complete each sentence with the correct form of the word given before each sentence. The word given is the form found in your reading. Refer to the word chart if necessary.

1 *laughingly* One of the most beautiful sounds in the world is the _____ of children.
The efforts of human beings to appear younger than they are are often _____.

2 *experienced* Many serious automobile accidents are caused by _____ drivers.
Those who have not yet _____ the death of a person close to them have not learned the meaning of grief.

3 *judgment*   A good _____ must be both objective and humane.
If we _____ others too harshly, we are not likely to have many friends.

4 *guilt*   In a criminal case, the accused is judged to be either innocent or _____.
The little boy who took money from his mother's purse looked about him _____ before replacing it where he had found it.

5 *danger-*
ous   People who drive while under the influence of alcohol _____ the lives of everyone else on public roads.
Those who live in earthquake zones live _____ whether they intend to or not.

The Blue Hotel
(Continued)

At supper that evening, the Swede burned with fierce energy. He sometimes seemed on the point of bursting into loud song, and in all of his madness he was encouraged by old Scully. The Easterner was quiet; the cowboy sat in wide-mouthed wonder, forgetting to eat, while Johnnie angrily finished great plates of food. The daughters of the house, when they were obliged to bring more bread, approached as carefully as rabbits. Having succeeded in their purpose, they hurried away with poorly-hidden fear. The Swede controlled the whole feast, and he gave it the appearance of a cruel affair. He seemed to have grown suddenly taller; he gazed bitterly into every face. His voice rang through the room.

After supper, as the men went toward the other room, the Swede hit Scully hard on the shoulder. "Well, old boy, that was a good meal."

Johnnie looked hopefully at his father. He knew the old man's shoulder was still painful from an old hurt. And indeed, it appeared for a moment as if Scully were going to flame out in anger about it. But Scully only smiled a sickly smile and remained silent. The others understood that he was admitting his responsibility for the Swede's new attitude.

When they were gathered about the stove, the Swede insisted on another game of cards. In his voice there was always a great threat. The cowboy and the Easterner both agreed, without interest, to play. Scully said that he would soon have to go to meet the evening train, and so the Swede turned to Johnnie. For a moment their glances crossed like swords, and then Johnnie smiled and said, "Yes, I'll play."

They formed a square around the table. The Easterner

and the Swede again played together. As the game continued, it was noticeable that the cowboy was not playing as noisily as before.

Scully left to meet the train. In spite of his care, an icy wind blew into the room as he opened the door. It scattered the cards and froze the players. The Swede cursed frightfully. When Scully returned, his icy entrance interrupted a comfortable and friendly scene. The Swede cursed again, but soon they were once more giving attention to their game, their heads bent forward and their hands moving fast.

Scully took up a newspaper, and as he slowly turned from page to page it made a comfortable sound. Then suddenly he heard three awful words: "You are cheating!"

The little room was now filled with terror. After the three words, the first sound in the room was made by Scully's paper as it fell forgotten to his feet. His eyeglasses had fallen from his nose, but by a grasp he had caught them. He stared at the card players.

Probably the silence was only an instant long. Then, if the floor had been suddenly pulled out from under the men, they could not have moved more quickly. The five had thrown themselves at a single point. Johnnie, as he rose to throw himself upon the Swede, almost fell. The loss of the moment allowed time for the arrival of Scully. It also gave the cowboy time to give the Swede a great push which sent him backwards. The men found voices together, and shouts of anger, appeal or fear burst from every throat. The cowboy pushed and pulled feverishly at the Swede, and the Easterner and Scully held wildly to Johnnie. But through the smoky air, above the straining bodies of the peace-compellers, the eyes of the enemies steadily warned each other.

Scully's voice was loudest. "Stop, now! Stop, I say! Stop, now—"

Johnnie, as he struggled to break away from Scully and the Easterner, was crying, "Well, he says I cheated! He says I cheated! I won't allow any man to say I cheated. If he says I cheated him, he's a—!"

The cowboy was telling the Swede, "Stop now! Stop, do you hear?"

The screams of the Swede never ceased: "He did cheat! I saw him! I saw him!"

As for the Easterner, he was begging in a voice that was not heard: "Wait a moment, can't you? Oh, wait a moment. What's the use of fighting over a game of cards? Wait a moment."

In this noisy quarrel, no complete sentence was clear. "Cheat" — "Stop" — "He says" — these pieces cut the screaming and rang out sharply. It was remarkable that Scully, who undoubtedly made the most noise, was the least heard.

Then suddenly there was a great stillness. It was as if each man had paused for breath. Although the room was still filled with the anger of men, it could be seen that there was no danger of immediate fighting.

At once Johnnie pushed forward. "Why did you say I cheated? Why did you say I cheated? I don't cheat, and I won't let any man say I do!"

The Swede said, "I saw you! I saw you!"

"Well," cried Johnnie, "I'll fight any man who says I cheat!"

"No, you won't," said the cowboy. "Not here."

Johnnie spoke to the Swede again. "Did you say I cheated?"

The Swede showed his teeth. "Yes."

"Then," said Johnnie, "we must fight."

"Yes, fight," roared the Swede. He was like a mad devil. "Yes, fight! I'll show you what kind of man I am! I'll show you who you want to fight! Maybe you think I can't fight! Maybe you think I can't! I'll show you, you criminal! Yes, you cheated! You cheated!"

"Well, let's start, then, fellow," said Johnnie coolly.

The cowboy turned in despair to Scully. "What are you going to do now?"

A change had come over the old man. He now seemed all eagerness; his eyes glowed.

"We'll let them fight," he answered bravely. "I can't watch this any longer. I've endured this cursed Swede till I'm sick. We'll let them fight."

The men prepared to go out. The Easterner was so nervous that he had great difficulty putting on his new leather coat. As the cowboy pulled his fur cap down over his ears, his hands trembled. In fact, Johnnie and old Scully were the only ones who displayed no emotion. No words were spoken during these proceedings.

Scully threw open the door. Instantly a wild wind caused the flame of the lamp to struggle for its life. The men lowered their heads and pushed out into the cold.

No snow was falling, but great clouds of it, swept up from the ground by the fierce winds, were streaming all around. The covered land was a deep blue, and there was no other color except one light shining from the low, black railroad station. It looked like a tiny jewel.

The Swede was calling out something. Scully went to him, put a hand on his shoulder, and indicated an ear. "What did you say?" he shouted.

"I said," screamed the Swede again, "I won't have a chance against this crowd. I know you'll all jump on me."

"No, no, man —" called Scully. But the wind tore the words from his lips and scattered them far.

The Swede shouted a curse, but the storm also seized the remainder of the sentence.

The men turned their backs upon the wind, and walked to the sheltered side of the hotel. Here a V-shaped piece of icy grass had not been covered by the snow. When they reached the spot, it was heard that the Swede was still screaming.

"Oh, I know what kind of a thing this is! I know you'll jump on me. I can't beat you all!"

Scully turned on him angrily. "You won't have to beat all of us. You'll have to beat my son Johnnie. And the man that troubles you during that time will have to deal with me."

The arrangements were quickly made. The two men faced each other, obeying the short commands of Scully. The Easterner was already cold and he was jumping up and down. The cowboy stood rock-like.

The fighters had not removed any clothing. Their hands were ready, and they eyed each other in a calm way that had the elements of fierce cruelty in it.

"Now!" said Scully.

The two leaped forward and struck like oxen. There was heard the dull sounds of blows, and of a curse pressed out between the tight teeth of one.

As for the watchers, the Easterner's held-in breath burst from him in relief, pure relief after the anxious waiting. The cowboy leaped into the air with a scream. Scully stood unmoving, as if in complete surprise and fear at the fierceness of the fight which he himself had permitted and arranged.

For a time the fight in the darkness was such a scene of flying arms that it showed no more detail than a moving wheel. Sometimes a face would shine out, frightful and marked with pink spots. A moment later, the men would be only shadows.

Suddenly the cowboy was caught by warlike desires, and he leaped with the speed of a wild horse. "Hit him, Johnnie! Hit him! Kill him! Kill him!"

"Keep still," said Scully icily.

Then there was a sudden sound, dull, incomplete, cut short. Johnnie's body fell away from the Swede, with sickening heaviness to the grass. The cowboy hardly had time to prevent the mad Swede from throwing himself upon the fallen body.

Scully was at his son's side. "Johnnie! Johnnie, my boy!" His voice had a quality of sad tenderness. "Johnnie! Can you fight some more?" He looked anxiously down into the bloody, beaten face of his son.

There was a moment of silence. And then Johnnie answered in his ordinary voice, "Yes — I — it — yes."

Helped by his father, he struggled to his feet. "Wait a minute now till you get your breath," said the old man.

A few steps away, the cowboy was telling the Swede, "No, you don't. Wait a second."

The Easterner was pulling at Scully's arm. "Oh, this is enough!" he begged. "This is enough! Let it go as it is. This is enough!"

"Bill," said Scully, "get out of the way." The cowboy stepped aside. "Now."

The fighters advanced toward each other. Then the Swede aimed a lightning blow that carried with it his entire weight. Johnnie, though faint from weakness, luckily stepped aside, and the unbalanced Swede fell to the ground.

The cowboy, Scully and the Easterner cheered, but before its finish the Swede was up, and attacking his enemy madly. There were more wildly moving arms and Johnnie's body again fell away, like a stone.

The Swede quickly struggled to a little tree and leaned upon it, breathing hard, while his fierce and flame-lit eyes wandered from face to face as the men bent over Johnnie.

"Can you still fight, Johnnie?" asked Scully in a voice of despair.

After a moment the son answered, "No — I can't — fight — any — more." Then, from shame and bodily ill, he began to weep, the tears pouring down through the blood on his face. "He was too — too — heavy for me."

Scully straightened and spoke to the waiting figure. "Stranger," he said calmly, "we're finished." Then his voice changed into that deep and quiet tone which is the tone of the most simple and deadly announcements. "Johnnie is beaten."

Without replying, the winner moved away to the front door of the hotel. The others raised Johnnie from the ground, and, as soon as he was on his feet, he refused all attempts at help. When the group came around the corner they were almost blinded by the blowing snow. It burned their faces like fire. The cowboy carried Johnnie through the piles of snow to the door.

Inside they were greeted by a warm stove and excited women who took Johnnie to the kitchen. The three others sat around the heat, and the sad quiet was broken only by the sounds overhead when the Swede moved about in his room.

Soon they heard him on the stairs. He threw open the door and walked straight to the middle of the room. No one looked at him. "Well," he said loudly to Scully, "I suppose you'll tell me now how much I owe you?"

The old man, with a dull expression, remained calm. "You don't owe me anything."

"Mr Scully," called the Swede again, "how much do I owe you?" He was dressed to go, and he had his bag in his hand.

"You don't owe me anything," repeated Scully in the same unmoved way.

"I guess you're right. I guess the truth would be that you would owe me something. That's what I guess." He turned to the cowboy. "Kill him! Kill him! Kill him!" he repeated, in the tone the cowboy had used. Then he laughed.

But he might have been laughing at the dead. The three men did not move or speak — just stared with glassy eyes at the stove.

The Swede opened the door and passed into the storm, giving one last glance at the still group.

The Swede's face, fresh from Johnnie's blows, felt more pleasure than pain in the wind and the whipping snow. A number of square shapes appeared before him and he recognised them as the houses of the town. He traveled along a street until he found a saloon. He pushed open a door and entered. At the end of the room four men sat drinking at a table.

The Swede dropped his bag upon the floor and, smiling at the saloon-keeper, said, "Give me some whiskey, will you?" The man placed a bottle, a whiskey glass, and a glass of ice-filled water upon a table. The Swede poured himself an extra large amount of whiskey and drank it down.

"Bad night," remarked the saloon-keeper, without interest. He was acting as though he were not noticing the man, but it could have been seen that he was secretly studying the remains of blood on the Swede's face. "Bad night," he said again.

"Oh, it's good enough for me," replied the Swede, as he poured himself some more whiskey. "No," continued the Swede, "this isn't too bad weather. It's good enough for me."

The large drinks of whiskey made the Swede's eyes watery, and he breathed a little heavier. "Well, I guess I'll take another drink," said the Swede after a while. "Would you like something?"

"No, thanks; I'm not drinking. How did you hurt your face?"

The Swede immediately began to talk loudly. "Oh, in a fight. I beat the soul out of a man at Scully's hotel."

This caught the interest of the four men at the table.

"Who was it?" asked one.

"Johnnie Scully, son of the man who owns the hotel. He will be nearly dead for some weeks, I can tell you. I beat him well, I did. He couldn't get up. They had to carry him into the house. Have a drink?"

Instantly the men in a quiet way surrounded themselves in privacy. "No, thanks," said one.

It was a strange group. Two were well-known local businessmen; one was a lawyer; and one was a gambler.

But a close look at the group would not have enabled an observer to pick the gambler from the other men. He was, in fact, so delicate in manner and so careful with whom he gambled that the men of the town completely trusted and admired him.

His business was regarded with fear and lack of respect. That is why, without doubt, his quiet dignity shone brightly above the quiet dignity of men who might be merely hat-makers, or builders or salesmen. Beyond an occasional unwise traveler who came by rail, this gambler supposedly cheated only careless farmers who, when rich with good crops, drove into town full of foolish pride. Hearing at times of such a farmer, the important men of Romper usually laughed at his losses. And if they thought of the gambler at all, it was with a kind of pride knowing he would never dare to attack their wisdom and courage.

Besides, it was known that this gambler had a wife and two children in a nice little house, where he led a perfect home life. And when anyone even suggested that there was a fault in his character, the men immediately described the virtues of his family life.

And one must not forget to declare the bare fact of his entire position in Romper. It is true that in all affairs other than his business, this card-player was so generous, so fair, so good, that he could be considered to have a higher moral sense than nine-tenths of the citizens of Romper.

And so it happened that he was seated in this saloon bar with two local businessmen and the lawyer.

The Swede continued to drink whiskey and to try to make the saloon-keeper drink with him. "Come on. Have a drink. Come on. No? Well, have a little one then. By God, I've beaten a man tonight, and I beat him good, too. Gentlemen," the Swede cried to the men at the table, "have a drink?"

"Ssh! Quiet!" said the saloon-keeper.

The group at the table, although really interested, had been trying to appear busy in talk. But now a man lifted his eyes toward the Swede and said shortly, "Thanks. We don't want any more."

At this reply, the Swede straightened. "Well," he shouted, "it seems I can't get anybody to drink with me. And I want someone to drink with me now. Now! Do you understand?" He struck the table with his hand.

Years of experience had hardened the saloon-keeper. He merely answered, "I hear you."

"Well," cried the Swede, "listen then. See those men over there? Well, they're going to drink with me, and don't you forget it. Now you watch."

"Stop that!" shouted the saloon-keeper.

"Why should I?" demanded the Swede. He walked to the men's table, and by chance laid his hand on the shoulder of the gambler. "What about it?" he asked angrily. "I asked you to drink with me."

The gambler simply turned his head and spoke over his shoulder. "My friend, I don't know you."

"Never mind!" answered the Swede. "Come and have a drink."

"Now, my boy," advised the gambler kindly, "take your hand off my shoulder and go away." He was a little, thin man and it seemed strange to hear him use this tone to the big Swede. The other men at the table said nothing.

"What! You won't drink with me, you little fool? I'll make you then! I'll make you." The Swede had grasped the gambler fiercely at the throat, and was dragging him from his chair. The other men jumped up. The saloon-keeper ran toward the table. There was a great scene of shouts and movements, and then a long knife appeared in the hand of the gambler. It shot forward, and a human body was cut as easily as if it had been a piece of fruit. The Swede fell with a cry of greatest surprise.

The businessmen and the lawyer must have rushed out of the place backward. The saloon-keeper found himself hanging weakly to the arm of a chair and gazing into the eyes of a murderer.

"Henry," said the latter, "you tell them where to find me. I'll be home waiting." Then he left. A moment afterward the saloon-keeper was in the street racing through the storm for help and, more important, companionship.

Months later, the cowboy was cooking meat on the stove of a small cattle farm near the Dakota border when there was the sound of a horse stopping outside. The Easterner entered with mail and newspapers.

"Well, said the Easterner at once, "the fellow who killed the Swede will spend three years in prison. That's not much, is it?"

"He will? Three years!" The cowboy turned the meat in the pan. "Three years. That isn't much."

"No," replied the Easterner. "There was a lot of sympathy for him in Romper."

"If the saloon-keeper had been any good," said the cowboy thoughtfully, "he would have gone in and hit that Swede on the head with a bottle in the beginning of it. That would have stopped all this murdering."

"Yes, a thousand things might have happened," said the Easterner sharply.

The cowboy moved his pan of meat on the fire, and continued with his philosophy. "It's strange, isn't it? If he hadn't said Johnnie was cheating, he'd be alive this minute. He was an awful fool. I believe he was crazy."

"I feel sorry for that gambler," said the Easterner.

"So do I," said the cowboy. "He doesn't deserve three years in prison for killing that fellow."

"The Swede might not have been killed if everything had been honest."

"Might not have been killed?" exclaimed the cowboy. "Everything honest? When he said that Johnnie was cheating and acted so crazy? And then in the saloon he practically asked to get hurt?" With these arguments the cowboy made the Easterner angry.

"You're a fool!" cried the Easterner fiercely. "You're a bigger fool than that Swede. Now let me tell you one thing. Let me tell you one thing. Let me tell you one thing. Listen! Johnnie was cheating!"

"Johnnie," said the cowboy, blankly. There was a minute of silence, and then he said strongly, "Oh, no. The game was only for fun."

"Fun or not," said the Easterner, "Johnnie was cheating. I saw him. I know it. I saw him. And I refused to stand up and be a man. I let the Swede fight alone. And you — you were simply jumping around the place and wanting to fight. And old Scully too! We are all in it! This poor gambler just got pulled into it. Every sin is the result of shared effort. We, five of us, have shared in the murder of this Swede. You, I, Johnnie, old Scully; and that fool of an unfortunate gambler came merely at the end of a human movement, and gets all the punishment."

The cowboy, hurt and angry, cried out blindly into this mystery of thought: "Well, I didn't do anything, did I?"

COMPREHENSION QUESTIONS

EXERCISE 1 For each question, write down the letter that corresponds to the correct answer. Choose only one.

1 How did the Swede control the meal that evening?
   (a) By his energy, his voice and his bitter gaze.
   (b) By ordering the daughters what to bring and when.
   (c) By telling Scully exactly what to do.
   (d) By getting Scully's encouragement.

2 Why did Johnnie look hopeful when the Swede hit his father hard on the shoulder?
   (a) Because Johnnie wanted his father to feel pain.
   (b) Because Johnnie hoped that this would turn Scully against the Swede.
   (c) Because he hoped that it meant that the Swede was no longer frightened.
   (d) Because he thought his father might now kill the Swede.

3 What did Scully's silence and sickly smile mean to the others?
   (a) That he had drunk too much whiskey.
   (b) That he was now frightened of the Swede.
   (c) That his health was not good.
   (d) That he admitted responsibility for the Swede's new attitude.

4 As Scully went and returned from the station, why did the Swede curse?
   (a) Because there were no new guests for the hotel.
   (b) Because Scully didn't bring any more whiskey with him.
   (c) Because an icy wind entered when the door was opened.
   (d) Because by cursing he could make Scully fear him.

5. What effect did the words, "You are cheating!", have on the room?
   (a) It was filled with terror.
   (b) It was filled with shocked laughter.
   (c) It was filled with curses and shouting.

    (d) It was filled with angry denials.

6 What did everyone want to do?
    (a) Leave the room immediately.
    (b) Keep Johnnie and the Swede separated.
    (c) Kill the Swede.
    (d) Quiet down and start the game again.

7 What argument did the Easterner use in trying to get the
  two enemies to stop fighting?
    (a) He said that all men were brothers.
    (b) He reminded them that no one had lost any money.
    (c) He told them that they were behaving badly in a public
        hotel.
    (d) He said that there was no purpose in fighting over a
        game of cards.

8 Why was it remarkable that Scully was the least heard?
    (a) Because he made the most noise.
    (b) Because he was the oldest and most respected.
    (c) Because he was the only one talking in complete
        sentences.
    (d) Because usually everyone listened to him carefully.

9 Who was opposed to a fight between Johnnie and the
  Swede?
    (a) Scully.
    (b) Everyone.
    (c) The cowboy.
    (d) The Easterner.

10 Why had a change come over Scully?
    (a) Because he now decided he should support his son.
    (b) Because he was afraid of Johnnie.
    (c) Because he thought everyone would consider him a
        coward if he didn't let his son fight.
    (d) Because he was thoroughly tired of the Swede.

11 Why did the Swede not think he could win the fight with
  Johnnie?
    (a) Because he believed all the men would fight him.
    (b) Because he was much older than Johnnie.
    (c) Because he had drunk too much whiskey.
    (d) Because he was a poor fighter.

12 Where did the men decide to fight?
    (a) In front of the hotel.
    (b) By the railroad station where there was light.
    (c) On the sheltered side of the hotel.
    (d) On the road which was cleared of snow.

13 When the fight began, why did the Easterner's breath burst from him?
    (a) Because of the extreme cold.
    (b) Because he had been hit in the stomach by mistake.
    (c) Because he felt relief after the anxious waiting.
    (d) Because he was deeply frightened.

14 What did the cowboy do when Johnnie was struck and fell?
    (a) He hit the Swede himself.
    (b) He screamed "Kill him! Kill him!"
    (c) He stopped the Swede from attacking the fallen Johnnie.
    (d) He ran away in fear.

15 When Johnnie resumed the fight, why did the Swede fall?
    (a) Because his blow missed Johnnie and he lost his balance.
    (b) Because he was very tired from all the activity.
    (c) Because Johnnie hit him with a lightning blow.
    (d) Because he was still drunk from the whiskey.

16 When Johnnie admitted defeat, what did he do?
    (a) He got up and walked slowly into the hotel.
    (b) He tried to wash the blood on his face.
    (c) He cried and said the Swede was too heavy for him.
    (d) He cursed his father for not putting the Swede out of the hotel.

17 Why did the Swede not insist on paying the hotel-keeper anything?
    (a) Because Scully refused to accept money.
    (b) Because the Swede, in fact, had almost no money.
    (c) Because Scully was very sad and the Swede didn't want to disturb him.
    (d) Because the Swede decided that Scully owed him something.

18 Where did the Swede go when he left the hotel?

(a) To the first door he saw in town.
(b) To the railroad station.
(c) To another hotel.
(d) To a saloon.

19 What did the saloon-keeper secretly notice about the Swede?
(a) That his face had blood on it.
(b) That his eyes were watery.
(c) That his breathing was heavy.
(d) That he was drunk.

20 What caught the interest of the four men at the table?
(a) The Swede's offer of a drink.
(b) The blood on his face.
(c) The great amount of whiskey he was drinking.
(d) His remark that he had beaten a man in a fight.

21 Why did the men of the town trust and admire the gambler?
(a) Because you couldn't tell him from other men.
(b) Because he was very rich.
(c) Because he had a delicate manner and was careful with whom he gambled.
(d) Because he always loaned people money who were in need.

22 How high a moral sense was the gambler considered to have?
(a) He was the best citizen in Romper.
(b) He cheated farmers and strangers.
(c) He was as normal as the average citizen of Romper.
(d) He was among the best 10 per cent.

23 Why did the saloon-keeper shout at the Swede?
(a) Because the Swede was drinking too much.
(b) Because the Swede did not seem to be listening to him.
(c) Because he liked Johnnie and was angry with the Swede.
(d) Because the Swede was disturbing his other customers.

24 Why did it seem strange to hear the gambler say, "Take your hand off my shoulder and go away," to the Swede?
(a) Because the gambler was a small, thin man.

(b) Because it was an impolite thing to say.

(c) Because he had never before refused an offer of a drink.

(d) Because he usually said nothing in such situations.

25 How did the gambler stop the fight?
   (a) By pushing the Swede to the floor.
   (b) By rushing out of the saloon backward.
   (c) By accepting the offer of a drink.
   (d) By killing the Swede with a knife.

26 When the saloon-keeper ran into the street, what was the most important thing he was looking for?
   (a) The gambler's home.
   (b) The police.
   (c) The businessmen.
   (d) Some companionship.

27 Months later, where were the Easterner and the cowboy?
   (a) On a cattle farm near Romper.
   (b) In the saloon in Romper.
   (c) Near the Dakota border on a farm.
   (d) The story doesn't say.

28 How did the cowboy think the saloon-keeper might have stopped the murder?
   (a) By grabbing the gambler's hand with the knife in it.
   (b) By refusing to sell the Swede any whiskey.
   (c) By hitting the Swede with a bottle.
   (d) By agreeing to have a drink with the Swede.

29 Why did the cowboy change his mind and say that the gambler didn't deserve three years in prison for killing the Swede?
   (a) Because he thought that the Swede was a fool and crazy.
   (b) Because he didn't really believe that he had killed him.
   (c) Because the Easterner had made him feel sorry for the gambler.
   (d) Because he had joined the Easterner in feeling sorry for the gambler.

30 What was the cowboy's first reaction when the Easterner said that Johnnie was, in fact, cheating?

(a) He said that the card game had not been serious.
(b) He said that Johnnie had never cheated,
(c) He said that the Easterner was a liar.
(d) He stared at the Easterner in disbelief.

31 Why did the Easterner feel ashamed of himself?
(a) Because he had not accused Johnnie of cheating when
he saw it.
(b) Because if he had been a real man he would not have
allowed the Swede to fight alone.
(c) Because he didn't leave the hotel when the Swede did.
(d) Because he had not told Scully that his son was a cheat.

32 In what way did the Easterner believe that all five of them
were responsible for the Swede's death?
(a) Because none of them had acted correctly.
(b) Because everyone was more interested in fighting than
in peaceful relations.
(c) Because according to him, all sin is the result of shared
effort.
(d) Because he believed that all men are brothers.

QUESTIONS FOR DISCUSSION AND WRITING PRACTICE

EXERCISE 2 The following may be used for classroom
discussion, for written homework, or for both.

1 Describe the different ways that the guests behaved at
supper in the hotel.

2 How did the Swede control the group?

3 Why did Scully look at the others with a sickly smile and
remain silent?

4 Describe the scene immediately after the Swede accused
Johnnie of cheating. Why is a charge of cheating taken so
seriously?

5 Why did Scully decide to let his son and the Swede fight?

6 As the fight progressed, what change came over the
cowboy?

7 What effect did the words "Kill him! Kill him!" have on the Swede?

8 How did Johnnie and Scully accept the defeat?

9 Describe the saloon-keeper and the other customers in the saloon.

10 What was the gambler's reputation? How does the writer use the gambler to reveal his own feelings about small-town citizens?

11 What did the people in the saloon do when the gambler killed the Swede? Why did they behave this way?

12 Why did the cowboy first agree that three years in prison wasn't much, and then later say that the gambler didn't deserve three years in prison? Is this the first time that the cowboy has shown himself to be of a changeable nature?

13 Why had the Easterner not said earlier that Johnnie had cheated?

14 What was the Easterner's philosophy about "sin"? How did the cowboy react to it?

15 What would you have done if you had been in the Easterner's place?

SYNONYMS

EXERCISE 3 For each question, write down the letter that corresponds to the correct synonym for the word(s) in italics.

1 At supper that night, the Swede burned with fierce *energy*.
   (a) strong (b) vitality (c) ambition (d) vigorous

2 By his silence, Scully *admitted* his responsibility for the Swede's new attitude.
   (a) acknowledged (b) allowed (c) received (d) entered

3 The icy wind *scattered* the cards and froze the players.
   (a) sowed (b) shook (c) turned (d) dispersed

4 The eyes of the enemies steadily *warned* each other.
   (a) endangered (b) hated (c) cautioned (d) stared at

5 "You won't have to *beat* all of us," said Scully to the Swede.
(a) strike (b) stir (c) box (d) defeat

6 The fighters *advanced toward* each other.
(a) approached (b) marched against (c) attacked (d) moved straight

7 The Swede aimed a *lightning* blow that carried with it his entire weight.
(a) electric (b) swift (c) shocking (d) stormy

8 When Johnnie got to his feet, he *refused* all offers of help.
(a) negative (b) didn't like (c) declined (d) deny

9 The sad quiet was *broken* only by the sounds overhead when the Swede moved about in his room.
(a) smashed (b) cracked (c) opened (d) interrupted

10 An observer could not have *picked* the gambler from the other men.
(a) selected (b) removed (c) gathered (d) observed

WORD STUDY

EXERCISE 4 Study these words and the sentences that follow them. If possible, repeat them after your teacher. The word in italics in the table is the form found in your reading.

WORD TABLE

	ADJECTIVE	NOUN	VERB	ADVERB
1	forgetful, unforgettable	forgetfulness	*forget*	forgetfully
2	sick, *sickly*, sickened, sickening	sickness	sicken	sickeningly
3	eager	*eagerness*		eagerly
4	weak, weakened	*weakness*, weakling	weaken	weakly

ADJECTIVE	NOUN	VERB	ADVERB
5 interesting, uninteresting, interested, uninterested	*interest,* disinterest	interest	interestingly, uninterestingly, interestedly

1 The cowboy sat in open-mouthed wonder, *forgetting* to eat. The quarrel between the Swede and Johnnie made the cowboy *forgetful* about the meal in front of him. He ate *forgetfully*. His *forgetfulness* on that occasion was unusual, because he normally ate well. The growing argument between the two enemies was an *unforgettable* experience for the cowboy.

2 Scully smiled a *sickly* smile and remained silent. He was growing *sick* of the Swede and regretted his kindness to him. His sense of responsibility for the Swede's new attitude gave him a feeling of *sickness* in his spirit. The thought of his own foolishness in encouraging the Swede to stay in the hotel *sickened* him. He thought *sickeningly* that his foolishness had caused a lot of trouble. Scully's *sickened* look showed that he accepted responsibility for the trouble.

3 A change had come over the old man and he now seemed all *eagerness*. He was *eager* to see his son fight the Swede. He looked forward *eagerly* to the fight.

4 Johnnie, though faint from *weakness*, luckily stepped aside. The strenuous fighting made him *weak*. Once *weakened*, Johnnie could no longer fight with any force. The Swede's heavy blows *weakened* the boy. Once the Swede had knocked him down, Johnnie fought *weakly*. When beaten, he believed that he was only a *weakling*.

5 The Swede's remark that he had beaten Johnnie caught the *interest* of the four men at the table. The remark *interested* them. The Swede was an *interesting* character, even though he wasn't likeable. In the small town of Romper, life often seemed *uninteresting*. Now, the four men pretended to be *uninterested*, but, in fact, they were all curious and *interested* in what the Swede was saying. They

could not keep up the pretense of *disinterest* for very long.
They listened *interestedly* as the Swede told of beating the
Scully boy severely. The Swede spoke *interestingly* in his
excitable way. Most of the people who came to the saloon
spoke *uninterestingly* of everyday, boring affairs.

Complete each sentence with the correct form of the word
given before each sentence. The word given is the form found
in your reading. Refer to the word chart if necessary.

1 *forget*   The birth of a first child is an _____ experience for both parents.
As people grow older, they tend to become more
_____.

2 *sickly*   The sight of a fatal automobile accident can
_____ even those with strong stomachs.
When the dentist pulls a tooth from your mouth,
the sound inside your head is _____.

3 *eagerness*   All students look forward to school holidays
_____.
Few people remain as _____ in their old
age as they were in their youth.

4 *weakness*   A _____ in a group of children is often
threatened and abused by the larger children.
Without food and water, human beings
_____ very quickly.

5 *interest*   It is hard to concentrate on what an
_____ teacher is saying.
In these days, space travel and speed of any kind
_____ young people.

Jack London

JACK LONDON, born on January 12, 1876, in San Francisco, spent his time among sailors in his youth and at fifteen years of age headed a band of oyster pirates. A year later, on a sealing vessel, he established his position by fist fights. In 1893 he tried to settle down, but the monotony of factory work drove him to wander as a tramp. Arrested, he reformed, attended high school, and studied five months at the University of California. In 1897 he joined the gold rush to the Klondike region of northwest Canada and Alaska, an experience affording materials for his first stories. By 1900 his fame was assured. In 1904 he was a correspondent in the Russo-Japanese War, and in 1907 he began a sailing voyage around the world, but in Australia he contracted a rare disease and was forced to return home.

His last years were clouded by depression. He died on November 20, 1916.

The story included here, "Love of Life," is taken from the collection *Love of Life and Other Stories* (1907), among which are some of his best Alaskan tales and some of his best writing.

Love of Life
by Jack London

The two men moved painfully down the bank and fell among the rocks that were scattered everywhere. They were tired and weak. Their faces showed the patient appearance that results from difficulty long endured. They were heavily burdened with blanket packs which were tied to their shoulders. Each man carried a gun. They walked in a leaning position, the shoulders forward, the head farther forward, the eyes fixed upon the ground.

"I wish we had a couple of those cartridges that are lying in our cache," said the second man.

His voice was completely without expression. And the first man, walking into the milky stream that flowed over the rocks, made no reply.

The other man followed at his heels. They did not remove their shoes, although the water was icy cold. It was so cold that their feet soon were without feeling. In places, the water dashed against their knees, and both men found it difficult to remain standing.

The man who followed slipped on a smooth rock and nearly fell. He recovered his footing with great effort, at the same time uttering a sharp cry of pain. He seemed faint and stretched one hand forward, seeking support against the air. When he had steadied himself, he stepped forward. But he slipped again and nearly fell. Then he stood still and looked at the other man, who had never turned his head.

The man stood still for fully a minute, as if he were deciding something. Then he called.

"I say, Bill, I hurt my foot."

Bill struggled ahead through the milky water. He did not

look around. The man watched him go, and although his face lacked expression, as before, his eyes had the look of a wounded animal.

The other man climbed the farther bank of the stream and continued straight ahead without looking back. The man in the stream watched him. His lips trembled a little.

"Bill!" he cried.

It was the despairing cry of a strong man in trouble, but Bill's head did not turn. The man watched him go, struggling forward up the hill toward the skyline. He watched him go until he passed over the hill-top and disappeared. Then he turned his gaze and slowly examined the circle of the world that remained to him now that Bill was gone.

The sun was low in the sky, almost hidden by a cover of clouds. The man looked at his watch, while supporting his weight on one leg. It was four o'clock in the afternoon. The season was near the end of July or the first of August. He did not know the exact date within a week or two, but that was enough to know that the sun marked the northwest.

He looked to the south and decided that somewhere beyond those hills lay the Great Bear Lake. Also, he knew that behind the same hills the Arctic Circle cut its way across the plains of northern Canada, called the Barrens. This stream in which he stood flowed into the Coppermine River, which in turn flowed north and emptied into the Arctic Ocean. He had never been there, but he had seen it once on a map.

Again his gaze completed the circle of the world about him. It was not a cheerful sight. Everywhere was soft skyline. The hills were all low-lying. There were no trees, no grasses. There was nothing but a vast emptiness that brought fear into his eyes.

"Bill!" he whispered, once and twice, "Bill!"

He stood trembling in the milky water, feeling the vastness pressing in upon him with great force. He began to shake as with a disease, until the gun falling from his hand into the stream brought him back to reality. He fought with his fear and, regaining his self-control, he recovered the gun from the water. He pushed his pack more toward his left shoulder. This helped to take a portion of its weight off the foot he had hurt. Then he proceeded slowly and carefully in great pain, to the bank of the stream.

He did not stop. With a worry that was madness, unmindful of the pain, he hurried up the hill to the top, over which his companion had disappeared. But at the top he saw a valley, empty of life. He fought with his fear again and won. Then once more he moved the pack further toward his left shoulder and struggled down the hill.

The bottom of the valley was very wet. Thick plant life held the moisture close to the surface and the water flowed from under his feet at every step. He picked his way carefully across the valley and followed the other man's footsteps along the rocks which made small islands in a sea of wet plant life.

Although alone, he was not lost. Farther on, he knew, he would come to where dead pine trees bordered the shore of a little lake. In the language of that country it was called the "land of little sticks." Into the lake flowed a small stream, the water of which was not milky. There was grass along that stream, but no trees. He would follow the stream until it divided. He would cross this place of dividing to another stream, flowing to the west. This he would follow until it emptied into the river Dease. Here he would find a cache under an upturned boat and covered with many rocks. In this cache there would be cartridges for his empty gun, and fish-hooks and lines.

Everything he needed for catching food would be there. Also he would find flour, a little meat, and some beans.

Bill would be waiting for him there, and they would find a boat and row south down the Dease to the Great Bear Lake. And south across the lake they would go, ever south, until they came to the Mackenzie River. And south, always south they would go, while the winter raced after them and the ice formed in the streams, and the days grew cold. South they would go, to some warm place where the trees grew tall and full and there was food without end.

These were the thoughts of the man as he struggled forward. But as strongly as he struggled with his body, he struggled equally with his mind. He tried to believe that Bill had not deserted him. Surely Bill would wait for him at the cache. He was forced to think this thought. Otherwise, there would not be any reason to continue, and he would lie down and die.

As the ball of the sun sank slowly into the northwest, he

recalled every inch of his and Bill's flight south ahead of the oncoming winter. And he thought again and again of the food in the cache. It had been two days since he had anything to eat. It was a far longer time since he had had enough to eat. Often he picked muskeg berries, put them into his mouth, and ate them. A muskeg berry is a small seed in a drop of water. In the mouth, the water melts away and the seed tastes bitter. The man knew there was no real food value in the berries; but he ate them patiently with a hope greater than his experience.

At nine o'clock that night he hit his toe on a rocky surface, and from weakness and tiredness he fell to the ground. He lay for some time, without movement, on his side. He took his pack from his back and dragged himself into a sitting position. It was not yet dark. While some light remained, he felt among the rocks for pieces of dried plants. When he had gathered a pile, he built a fire and put a tin pot of water on it to boil.

He unwrapped his pack. The first thing he did was to count his matches. There were 67. He counted them three times to be sure. He divided them into several portions, wrapping them in paper. He put one portion in his empty tobacco pack, another in the inside band of his hat, and a third under his shirt against his flesh. This accomplished, he began to worry whether he had counted correctly. He unwrapped them all and counted them again. Yes, there were 67.

He dried his wet shoes and socks by the fire. The moccasins were badly torn. His socks were worn through in places, and his feet were bleeding. The area between his foot and leg, the ankle, was very painful. He examined it. It had swelled until it was as large as his knee. He cut a long strip from one of his two blankets and bound the ankle tightly. He cut other strips and bound them about his feet to serve both for moccasins and socks. Then he drank the pot of hot water, wound his watch, and pulled his blankets around him.

He slept like a dead man. The brief darkness at midnight came and went. Then the sun rose in the northeast. It can better be said that day dawned in that quarter of the sky, because the sun was hidden by gray clouds.

At six o'clock in the morning he woke, quietly lying on his back. He gazed straight up into the gray sky and knew that he was hungry. As he lifted himself on his elbow, he was frightened by a loud noise. There was a caribou looking at him curiously. The animal was not more than 50 feet away, and instantly, into the man's mind came the picture of caribou meat cooking over a fire. From habit, he reached for the empty gun and aimed it. The caribou leaped away and disappeared across the rocks.

The man cursed and threw the empty gun on the ground. He uttered a cry of pain as he started to drag himself to his feet. It was a slow task. When he finally stood on his feet, he needed another minute or two to straighten himself, so that he could stand as a man should stand.

He climbed a small hill and looked about. There were no trees, no bushes. There was nothing but grassy gray plants and some gray rocks and gray streams. The sky was gray. There was no sun or promise of sun. He had no idea of where north was, and he had forgotten how he had come to this spot the night before. But he was not lost. He knew that. Soon he would come to the land of the little sticks. He felt that it lay to the left somewhere not far. Possibly it was over the next low hill.

He returned to prepare his pack for traveling. He assured himself of the existence of his three separate portions of matches, although he did not stop to count them. But he did pause, trying to decide what to do about a bag made from moose skin. It was not large. It could be covered by his two hands. But he knew that it weighed 15 pounds — as much as all the rest of the pack. This worried him. He finally set it to one side and proceeded to roll the pack. He paused again to gaze at the moose-skin bag. He picked it up quickly with a quick glance around him. It was as if he thought the cruel wasteland was trying to steal it. When he rose to his feet, the bag was included in the pack on his back.

He started walking to the left, stopping now and again to eat muskeg berries. His ankle had stiffened, but the pain of it was nothing compared with the pain of his stomach. His hunger was so great he could not keep his mind steady on the course he had to follow to arrive at the land of the little sticks. The berries did not help his hunger. Their bitter taste only made his tongue and mouth sore.

He came to a valley where some birds rose from the rocky places. "Ker-ker-ker" was the sound of their cry. He threw stones at them but could not hit them. He placed his pack on the ground and followed them as a cat advances on a bird. The sharp rocks cut through his trousers until his knees left a trail of blood. But the hurt was lost in the pain of his hunger. He moved his body through the wet plants, becoming wet and cold in the process. But he did not notice this, so great was his desire for food.

Always the birds rose before him. Their cry of "Ker-ker-ker" sounded as if they were laughing at him. He cursed them and cried aloud at them with their own cry.

Once he came upon one that must have been asleep. He did not see it until it flew up in his face from behind some rocks. He grasped the air as suddenly as the rise of the bird and there remained in his hand three tail feathers. As he watched its flight he hated it. He felt that it had done him some great wrong. Then he returned to where he had left his pack and lifted it again to his back.

As the day continued, he came into valleys where game was plentiful. Twenty or more caribou passed by, within easy shooting distance of a gun. He felt a wild desire to run after them, certain that he could catch them. A small black animal came toward him, carrying a bird in its mouth. The man shouted. It was a fearful cry, but the animal, leaping away in fright, did not drop the bird.

Late in the afternoon he followed a stream which flowed through some thick grass. He grasped these grasses firmly near the root and pulled up what looked like a vegetable. It was round and white. Eagerly he sank his teeth into it. It was tender on the outside and gave the promise of food. But its inside was hard and stringy and, like the berries, it had no food value. Nevertheless, he threw off his pack and went among the grasses on his hands and knees, eating the grass like a cow.

He was very tired and often wished to rest — to lie down and sleep. But he was led on, not so much by his desire to find the land of the little sticks as by his hunger.

He looked into every pool of water, searching without success for things to eat. Then, as the night darkened, he discovered a single small fish in one of these pools. He plunged his whole arm in, but the fish escaped his grasp. He reached for it with both hands and stirred the mud at the bottom of the pool. During his excitement he fell in, getting wet as high as his shoulders. Then the water was too cloudy with mud and to allow him to see the fish. He was forced to wait until the mud had again settled to the bottom.

Then he tried again, until the water was again filled with mud. But he could not wait. He took a tin container from his pack and began to empty the water from the pool. He threw it out wildly at first, and so short a distance that it flowed into the pool again. He worked more carefully, trying to be calm, but his head was pounding and his hands were trembling. At the end of half an hour the pool was nearly dry. Not a cupful of water remained. And there was no fish.

Then he discovered a narrow opening among the stones through which it had escaped into a larger pool — a pool which he could not empty in a night and a day. If he had known of the opening, he could have closed it with a rock before he began and the fish would have been his.

Thus he thought, and he sank down upon the wet earth. At first he cried softly to himself. Then he cried loudly to the uncaring wasteland around him.

He built a fire and warmed himself by drinking hot water. Then he built a camp on the rocks as he had done the night before. The last things he did were to be certain that his matches were dry and to wind his watch. The blankets were wet. His ankle pained him. But he knew only that he was hungry. Through his restless sleep he dreamed of feasts and of food served in all imaginable manners.

When he awakened he was cold and sick. There was no sun. The gray of earth and sky had become deeper. A cold wind was blowing and snow was whitening the hill-tops. The air about him grew white with snow while he made a fire and boiled more water. It was wet snow, half rain. At first it melted as soon as it hit the earth. But it continued falling, covering the ground and destroying his fire.

This was a signal for him to put his pack on his back and struggle forward, he knew not where. He was not concerned with the land of little sticks, nor with Bill and the cache under the upturned boat by the river Dease. He was mad because of hunger. He did not notice the course he followed, except that it led him through the wet snow to the watery muskeg berries, and he was guided by touch as he pulled up the grass by the roots.

But it had no taste and did not satisfy his hunger.

He had no fire that night, nor hot water. He pulled his blanket around him to sleep the broken sleep of hunger. The snow became a cold rain. He awakened many times to feel it falling on his upturned face.

Day came. It was a gray day with no sun. It had ceased raining. The sharpness of his hunger had departed. There was a dull pain in his stomach, but it did not trouble him so much. He was more in control of himself. And once again he was interested in the land of little sticks and the cache by the river Dease.

He cut the remains of one of his blankets into strips and bound his bleeding feet. He used one of the strips on his swelled ankle and prepared himself for a day of travel. When he was ready to pick up his pack, he paused long before deciding to keep the moose-skin bag, but when he departed, it went with him.

The snow had melted under the rain, and only the hill-tops showed white. The sun appeared and he succeeded in locating the way he had been traveling. But now he knew that he was lost. Perhaps he had wandered too far to the left. He now turned to the right to return to his true course.

Although the hunger pains were not as great as they had been, he realized that he was weak. He was forced to pause for frequent rests. At those times he ate the muskeg berries and grasses. His tongue felt dry and large and it tasted bitter in his mouth. His heart troubled him very much. When he had traveled a few minutes, it would begin pounding. Then it would leap in a series of beats that made him feel faint.

In the middle of the day he found two small fish in a large pool. It was impossible to empty it. But he was now calmer and he managed to catch them. They were no bigger than his little finger, but now he was not particularly hungry. The dull pain in his stomach had been growing duller. It almost seemed that his stomach was asleep. He ate the fish with great care. The eating was an act of pure reason. Although he had no desire to eat, he knew that he must eat to live.

In the evening he caught three more small fish, eating two and saving the third for breakfast. The sun had dried the wet plants and he was able to build a fire. He had not traveled more than ten miles that day. The next day, traveling whenever his heart permitted, he went no more than five miles. But his stomach did not give him any pain. It seemed to be sleeping. He was now in a strange country, too, and the caribou were becoming more plentiful. There were wolves also. Their howls could be heard across the land and once he saw three of them crossing his path.

(to be continued)

COMPREHENSION QUESTIONS

EXERCISE 1 For each question, write down the letter that corresponds to the right answer. Choose only one.

1 What had caused the patient expressions on the faces of the two tired men who fell among the rocks?
   (a) Their gentle natures.
   (b) Their hope of finding food.
   (c) Difficulty long endured.
   (d) Their heavy burdens.

2 Why did the man who followed Bill utter a cry of pain?
   (a) Because he had slipped among the rocks and hurt his foot.
   (b) Because the water was icy cold.
   (c) Because of the heavy burden on his back.
   (d) Because the water dashed against his knees.

3 When Bill failed to turn around to help his injured companion, how did the companion react?
   (a) He refused to believe that Bill had heard him.
   (b) His eyes had the look of a wounded animal.
   (c) His face showed some expression which it had lacked earlier.
   (d) He cried out of grief and anger.

4 Where did Bill go?
   (a) Straight along through the bed of the stream.
   (d) He reversed himself and walked back where he had come from.
   (c) Toward the north.
   (d) Up the hill and over the hill-top.

5. How did the injured man know the geography of the area?
  (a) Because he had traveled over it many times.
  (b) Because Bill had told him about it.
  (c) Because he had once seen a map of the area.
  (d) Because he had come this way once before.

6 Why did he whisper Bill's name?
  (a) Because he hoped Bill would hear him and return.
  (b) Because the vast emptiness of the region brought fear into his eyes.
  (c) Because he was still angry that Bill had abandoned him.
  (d) Because Bill had been his best friend in all the world.

7 Why did he want to follow the stream that emptied into the river Dease?
  (a) Because the water was clear, not milky.
  (b) Because it was full of fish.
  (c) Because there was gold in it.
  (d) Because there he would find some hidden supplies.

8 Why did he want to go south?
  (a) Because Bill was there.
  (b) Because it was warmer and there would be food.
  (c) Because his home was in the south.
  (d) Because he disliked the cold weather of the north.

9 Why did he force himself to believe that Bill would wait for him at the cache?
  (a) Because Bill had promised to meet him there.
  (b) Because otherwise he might believe that Bill was dead.
  (c) Because otherwise his life would lose purpose and he would die.
  (d) Because Bill was a very reliable person.

10 How long had it been since he had had enough to eat?
  (a) Much longer than two days.
  (b) Two days.
  (c) Two weeks.
  (d) He couldn't remember.

11 In which of the following places did he not put any matches when he stopped to rest that night?
  (a) Under his shirt.

(b) Inside his hat band.
(c) In his tobacco pack.
(d) Inside one of his shoes.

12 When he awoke to a gray cloudy morning, what was the first thing that came into his mind?
(a) The thought of the injury to his ankle.
(b) The thought of his 67 matches.
(c) The thought of the cache on the river Dease.
(d) The thought of his hunger.

13 Although the man told himself that he was not lost, how do we know that he was?
(a) Because he didn't know where the land of the little sticks was.
(b) Because he didn't know where north was and he had forgotten how he had come the night before.
(c) Because there was no sun or promise of sun to guide him.
(d) Because he did not know what was over the next low hill.

14 Why was he worried about carrying a bag made from moose skin?
(a) Because it was very large.
(b) Because it would not fit into his pack.
(c) Because he feared someone might try to steal it.
(d) Because it weighed as much as all the rest of his pack.

15. When he hurt his knees following the birds that cried "Ker-ker-ker", why did he not notice the pain?
(a) Because he was very wet and cold.
(b) Because his legs were frozen.
(c) Because the pain was lost in his anger at the birds.
(d) Because the pain was lost in his hunger.

16 For what reason did he shout at the small animal with a bird in its mouth?
(a) Because it startled him.
(b) Because it ran into him and hurt him.
(c) Because he hoped it would drop the bird in fright.
(d) Because it had something to eat, whereas he had nothing.

17 When the man discovered that the small fish had escaped into a larger pool, what did he do?
  (a) He emptied the larger pool in a day and a night.
  (b) He fell into the larger pool trying to catch the fish.
  (c) He closed the opening of the small pool with a rock.
  (d) He cried, first softly, then loudly.

18 The next day, why didn't he notice the course that he followed?
  (a) Because it was snowing too hard to see anything.
  (b) Because the area was new to him.
  (c) Because he was already half blind.
  (d) Because he could think of nothing but food.

19 For three of the following reasons the morning after the wet, cold night was a little more comfortable. Which reason does not apply?
  (a) It had ceased raining.
  (b) He was not so hungry.
  (c) He was more in control of himself.
  (d) He knew where he was.

20 After wrapping his bloody feet and binding his ankle, what did the man decide to do with the moose-skin bag?
  (a) He took it with him.
  (b) He threw it away.
  (c) He emptied half of its contents and carried the rest.
  (d) He found a good hiding place and carefully hid it.

21 When he realized that he was lost, what did he do?
  (a) He turned to the left.
  (b) He turned to the right.
  (c) He returned the way he had come.
  (d) He went straight ahead.

22 How did he eat the two small fish which he managed to catch at midday?
  (a) Carefully but without hunger.
  (b) Greedily.
  (c) Rapidly.
  (d) Hungrily but carefully.

23 When he caught three more fish, why did he not eat all of them?

(a) Because he didn't like them.
(b) Because he had a great pain in his stomach.
(c) Because he wanted to save one for breakfast.
(d) Because one of them escaped into a larger pool.

QUESTIONS FOR DISCUSSION AND WRITING PRACTICE

EXERCISE 2 The following questions may be used for classroom discussion, for written homework, or for both.

1 Where were the two men going?

2 Why do you think Bill refused to return and help his companion?

3 Why were they anxious to reach their cache?

4 Why did the injured man force himself to think that Bill would wait for him at the cache?

5 Why did he count and divide his matches so carefully?

6 Describe the man's encounters with the sleeping bird, the small black animal, and the single small fish.

7 When preparing himself for a day of travel, why did the man pause before deciding to take the moose-skin bag with him?

8 What kind of country was he traveling through?

9 How did his heart trouble him?

10 Describe the way that he ate the small fish which he managed to catch.

11 Do you think that this man is unusual, or that most men would behave as he did under similar circumstances?

SYNONYMS

EXERCISE 3 For each question, write down the letter that corresponds to the correct synonym for the word(s) in italics.

1 The two men were heavily *burdened* with blanket packs which were tied to their shoulders.
   (a) troubled (b) loaded (c) carried (d) dressed

2 As the men walked, their eyes were *fixed* upon the ground.
   (a) attached (b) fastened (c) repaired (d) fallen

3 There was nothing but a *vast* emptiness that brought fear into his eyes.
   (a) high (b) silent (c) immense (d) frightening

4 The gun falling from his hand into the stream brought him back to *reality*.
   (a) actuality (b) wakefulness (c) solid (d) true

5 With a worry that was madness, *unmindful of* the pain, he hurried up the hill to the top.
   (a) ignoring (b) accustomed (c) aware (d) unaware

6 He tried to believe that Bill had not *deserted* him.
   (a) abandoned (b) escaped (c) injured (d) forgotten

7 There was a caribou looking at him *curiously*.
   (a) impolitely (b) frankly (c) inquisitively (d) madly

8 His hunger was so great he could not keep his mind *steady* on the course he had to follow.
   (a) sane (b) reliable (c) fixed (d) sober

9 The sharp rocks cut through his trousers until his knees left a *trail* of blood.
   (a) pool (b) track (c) road (d) string

10 He dreamed of food served in all *imaginable* manners.
   (a) magical (b) fairy-tale (c) fantastic (d) conceivable.

WORD STUDY

EXERCISE 4 Study these words and the sentences that follow them. If possible, repeat them after your teacher. The word in italics in the table is the form found in your reading.

WORD CHART

	ADJECTIVE	NOUN	VERB	ADVERB
1	*patient,* impatient	patience, impatience		patiently, impatiently
2	burdened, burdensome	burden	*burden,* unburden	
3	rested, restful, *restless*	rest, restlessness	rest	restfully, restlessly
4	sharp	*sharpness*	sharpen	sharply
5	*plentiful,*	plenty, plenitude		plentifully

1 The faces of the two men showed the *patient* appearance that results from difficulty long endured. They had been more *impatient* with their problems when they first left the north. Their *patience* was learned from hard experience. They found that *impatience* did not catch any fish or load an empty gun. They walked painfully and *patiently* as far as they could every day. When occasionally they moved *impatiently,* they found that they fell and hurt themselves.

2 They were heavily *burdened* with blanket packs which were tied to their shoulders. The *burdened* men walked in a leaning position, the shoulders forward, the head farther forward. One of the reasons why the load was so *burdensome* was the moose-skin bag which each man carried. Each man's *burden* would have been lightened by 15 pounds if he had thrown away this bag. At night, after a long hard day, the men longed to *unburden* themselves of their heavy loads.

3 Through his *restless* sleep he dreamed of feasts and of food served in all imaginable manners. For weeks he had not passed a truly *restful* night. He never felt *rested* anymore. He needed *rest* badly but none would come until he found food and shelter. His *restlessness* at night was caused from hunger and extreme fatigue. He could not *rest* until he

reached his destination in the south. He dreamed of times when he could sleep *restfully* in a comfortable bed in a warm house. Meanwhile, his hunger and urge to live drove him on *restlessly* towards the south.

4 The *sharpness* of his hunger had departed. The *sharp* pain in his stomach had turned into a dull ache. But his swollen ankle still pained him *sharply,* especially when he first stood up in the morning. The pain *sharpened* as he tried to stand on his feet after lying down all night.

5 He was now in a strange country, too, and the caribou were becoming more *plentiful.* There were *plenty* of animals to shoot for food if only he had had cartridges for his gun. Because there was grass and water, there was a *plenitude* of wild life of all kinds. The grassy wet land produced wild animals and fish *plentifully*.

Complete each sentence with the correct form of the word given before the sentence. The word given is the form found in your reading. Refer to the word chart if necessary.

1 *patient* A donkey owner knows that _____ will move a donkey faster than _____.
An old saying: _____ is a virtue.
Drivers who drive their cars _____ in crowded areas cause many serious accidents.

2 *burden* Old people who are ill and cannot work frequently feel that life is _____ .
When you feel sad and troubled, it is good to be able to _____ yourself to a friend.

3 *restless* When children sleep _____ at night, they are relaxed and happy during the day.
After a good vacation, our friends look _____ and refreshed.

4 *sharpness* Before an examination, good students _____ their wits as well as their pencils.
When the teacher caught the student cheating, he spoke very _____ to him.

5 *plentiful*   There is a _____ of good wines and
cheeses in France.
For thousands of years, the oceans have supplied
men _____ with fish.

Love of Life
(continued)

Another night passed. And in the morning, being more reasonable, he untied the leather string that held the moose-skin
bag. From its open mouth poured a yellow stream of gold
dust. He divided the gold into two equal parts. One half,
wrapped in a piece of a blanket, he hid among a large forma-
tion of rocks. The other half he returned to the bag. He also
began to use strips of the one remaining blanket for his feet.
He still kept his gun, because there were cartridges in that
cache by the river Dease.

This was a cloudy day, and this day hunger waked in him
again. He was very weak. It was no uncommon thing now for
him to fall. Once he fell into a bird's nest. There were four tiny
birds, a day or so old, no more than a mouthful. He ate them
greedily, putting them alive into his mouth and crushing them
like eggshells between his teeth. The mother bird flew about
him with cries of anger. He used his gun as a club with which
to hit her, but she flew beyond his reach. He threw stones at her
and by chance, one broke a wing. Then she ran away,
dragging the broken wing, with him following her.

The little birds had not satisfied his hunger. He jumped
along on his painful ankle. throwing stones and screaming
loudly at times. At other times, he struggled along silently,
picking himself up patiently when he fell, or rubbing his eyes
with his hand when faintness threatened to overpower him.

The bird led him across some wet ground in the bottom of
the valley. He discovered footprints in the wet grasses. They
were not his own. He could see that. They must be Bill's. But
he could not stop, because the mother bird was running
ahead. He would catch her first. Then he would return and

examine the footprints.

He tired the mother bird; but he tired himself also. She lay on her side breathing heavily. He lay on his side, a dozen feet away, unable to move toward her. And as he recovered, she recovered. She flew beyond reach as his hungry hand stretched out to catch her. The hunt started again. Night darkened and she escaped. He fell because of weakness, cutting his face. He did not move for a long time; then he rolled on his side. He wound his watch and lay there until morning.

It was another gray day. Half of his last blanket had been used for foot-wrapping. He failed to find Bill's trail again. It was not important. His hunger drove him on. He wondered if Bill, too, were lost. By the middle of the day, the weight of his pack became too great. Again he divided the gold, this time he merely poured half of it on the ground. In the afternoon he threw away the rest of it. There remained now only the half of the blanket, the tin container and the gun.

A hallucination began to trouble him. He felt certain that one cartridge remained. It was in his gun and he had not seen it. However, he knew all the time that the gun was empty. But the hallucination continued. He fought it for hours. Then, he opened his gun eagerly, only to find nothing inside.

He struggled ahead for half an hour, when the hallucination arose again. Again he fought it, and still it continued. To give himself relief, he again opened the gun and found it empty.

At times his mind wandered ever further. But these moments away from reality were brief, because always the pains of hunger forced him to return. Once, as his mind was wandering, he was returned to reality by a sight that almost caused him to faint. Before him stood a horse. A horse! He could not believe his eyes. A thick cloud was in his eyes. flashing with points of light. He rubbed his eyes fiercely to clear his sight. Then he saw before him not a horse, but a great brown bear. The animal was studying him with curiosity.

The man had brought his gun half the distance to his shoulder before he realized what he was doing. He lowered it and drew his hunting knife from its cover. Before him was meat and life. He ran his finger along the edge of his knife. It was sharp. The point was sharp. He would throw himself upon the bear and kill it. But his heart began its pounding. Then came its wild leap and he began to feel faint.

His wild courage was replaced by a great fear. In his weakness, what if the animal attacked him? He drew himself up tall, grasping the knife and staring hard at the bear. The bear advanced a couple of steps and stood up. If the man ran, the bear would run after him; but the man did not run. He was alive now with the courage of fear.

The bear moved away to one side with a threatening noise. He, himself, was fearful of this strange creature that appeared unafraid. But the man did not move. He stood still until the danger was past. Then he yielded to a fit of trembling and sank to his knees on the wet grass.

He regained control of himself and then started to move forward, afraid now in a new manner. It was not the fear that he would die from lack of food. He was afraid that he would be destroyed by forces other than starving. There were the wolves. Across the wasteland their howls could be heard, making the air itself a threat most real to him.

Now and again the wolves, in groups of two and three crossed his path. But they stayed away from him. They were not in sufficient numbers to attack, and besides, they were hunting caribou. Caribou did not battle, while this strange creature that walked on two legs might bite.

In the late afternoon he came upon scattered bones where the wolves had made a kill. What remained had been a young caribou an hour before. He studied the bones, cleaned of any flesh. They were still pink with the life in them which had not yet died. Might he look like that before the day was done? Was this life? A fleeting thing without meaning? It was only life that pained. There was no hurt in death. To die was to sleep. It meant rest. Then why was he not content to die?

But he did not think about these things for very long. He was soon seated in the grass, a bone in his mouth, biting at the bit of life that made it yet pink. The sweet meaty taste drove him mad. He closed his teeth firmly on the bones. Sometimes it was the bone that broke, sometimes his teeth. Then he crushed the bones between the rocks. He pounded them into tiny pieces, and ate them. He was in such a hurry that he pounded his fingers, too. He felt surprised at the fact that his fingers did not hurt much when they were caught under the rock.

Then came frightful days of snow and rain. He did not know when he made camp and when he broke camp. He traveled in the night as much as in the day. He rested whenever he fell, moving ahead whenever the dying life in him started up again. He, as a man, no longer struggled. It was the life in him, unwilling to die, that drove him on. He did not suffer, nor feel pain. But his mind was filled with hallucinations and wild dreams.

But he still ate the crushed bones of the young caribou, which he had gathered and carried with him. He crossed no more hills, but followed a large stream which flowed through a wide valley. He did not see this stream nor this valley. He saw nothing except hallucinations.

One morning he awakened with his mind clear, lying on his back on a rocky surface. The sun was shining bright and warm. Far away, he heard the noises made by young caribou. He remembered the rain and wind and snow, but whether he had been beaten by the storm for two days or two weeks he did not know.

For some time he lay without movement. The friendly sun poured down upon him and filled his body with its warmth. A fine day, he thought. Perhaps he could succeed in locating himself. By a painful effort he rolled on his side.

Below him flowed a wide river. Its unfamiliarity puzzled him. Slowly he followed it with his eyes, as it curved among the bare hills. They were more bare and lower than any hills he had yet seen. Slowly, without excitement, he followed the course of the strange stream toward the skyline and saw that it emptied into a bright and shining sea. He was still unexcited. Most unusual, he thought. It was probably a trick of his mind. He was certain of this when he also saw a ship floating in the shining sea. He closed his eyes for a while, then opened them. It was strange how the sight continued. Yet it was not strange. He knew there were no seas nor ships in the middle of this land, as he had known there was no cartridge in the empty gun.

He heard a noise behind him. It seemed like the dry sound that comes from the throat when air is forced out in a cough. Very slowly, because of his weakness and stiffness he rolled to his other side. He could see nothing near, but he waited patiently. Again came the cough, and there, between two rocks, he saw the gray head of a wolf. The sharp ears did not stand up as straight as he had seen them on other wolves. The eyes were dull and the head seemed to hang. The animal opened and shut its eyes frequently in the sunshine. It seemed sick. As he looked, it coughed again.

This was real, he thought. He turned on the other side to see the reality of the world which had been hidden from him before his hallucination. But the sea still shone and the ship was still there. Was it reality? He closed his eyes for a long while and thought, and then he remembered.

He had been traveling north by east, away from the Dease Divide and into the Coppermine Valley. This wide river was the Coppermine. That shining sea was the Arctic Ocean. That ship was a fishing boat which had wandered east from the mouth of the Mackenzie River. Now it was lying in Coronation Gulf. He remembered the map he had seen long ago, and it was all clear and reasonable to him.

He sat up and turned his attention to immediate affairs. He had worn holes through the blanket wrappings, and his feet were like shapeless pieces of meat. His last blanket was gone. His gun and knife were both lost. He had also lost his hat somewhere, with the matches in the band. The matches against his chest were safe and dry inside the paper. He looked at his watch. It marked eleven o'clock and was still going. This proved that he had kept it wound.

He was calm. Although very weak, he had no feeling of pain. He was not hungry. The thought of food was not even pleasant to him. Whatever he did was done entirely by reasoning. He tore off the legs of his trousers to the knees and bound them about his feet. Somehow he had succeeded in keeping the tin container. He would have some hot water before he began what he knew was to be an awful journey to the ship.

His movements were slow. He shook as if with disease. When he started to gather dried grasses he found he could not rise to his feet. He tried again and again. Then he contented himself with moving about on his hands and knees. Once he went near the sick wolf. The animal dragged itself out of the way, licking its face with a tongue which seemed hardly to have the strength to curl. The man noticed that the tongue was not the customary healthy red, but a yellowish-brown and covered with a half-dried coating.

After he drank some hot water, the man found he was able to stand. He could even walk as well as a dying man might be supposed to walk. But every minute or two he was forced to rest. His steps were unsteady, as were the steps of the wolf behind him. That night, when the shining sea was hidden in the blackness, he knew he was nearer to it by no more than four miles.

Through the night he heard the cough of the sick wolf and now and then, the noises of the young caribou. There was life all around him. But it was a strong life, very much alive and well. He knew the sick wolf was following the sick man's steps in the hope that the man would die first. In the morning, when he opened his eyes, he saw it looking at him with a hungry stare. It stood with its tail between its legs like an unhappy dog.

The sun rose brightly, and all morning the man headed toward the ship on the shining sea. The weather was perfect. It was the brief return of summer which was usual in that country. It might continue for a week. Or, tomorrow or the next day it might be gone.

In the afternoon the man came to a track. It was that of another man, who did not walk, but who dragged himself on his hands and knees. The man thought it might be Bill, but he thought about it without any interest. He had no curiosity. Feeling and emotion had left him. He was no longer able to feel pain. Yet the life that was in him drove him ahead. He was very tired, but it refused to die. It was because it refused to die that he still ate muskeg berries and small fish, drank hot water, and kept a careful eye on the sick wolf.

He followed the track of the other man who dragged himself along. Soon he came to the end of it. There were a few freshly cleaned bones where the grass was marked by the foot-prints of many wolves. He saw a moose-skin bag, exactly like his own. It had been torn by sharp teeth. He picked it up, although its weight was almost too much for his weak fingers. Bill had carried it to the end. Now he would have the last laugh. He would live and carry it to the ship in the shining sea. He laughed aloud, making an inhuman sound, and the sick wolf howled with him. The man ceased suddenly. How could he laugh at Bill, if that were Bill; if those bones, so pinky-white and clean, were Bill?

He turned away. Bill had deserted him. But he would not take the gold, nor would he eat Bill's bones. Bill would have done so, however, had their situations been exchanged.

He came to a pool of water. Bending over it in search of fish, he threw his head back as if he had been struck. He had caught sight of his face in the water. So awful was it that his feelings were stirred long enough to be shocked. There were three fish in the pool, which was too large to empty. After several attempts to catch them in his tin container, he stopped. He was afraid, because of his great weakness, that he might fall and sink into the water. It was for this reason, too, that he did not trust himself to ride down the river atop one of the many logs to be found along its banks.

That day he lessened the distance between him and the ship by three miles. The next day he traveled only two miles because he was now dragging himself on his hands and knees as Bill had done. At the end of the fifth day the ship was still seven miles away. He was unable to travel as much as a mile a day. However, the summer weather continued, and he continued to move toward the ship. And always the sick wolf coughed at his heels.

His knees had become red meat like his feet. Although he bound them with the shirt from his back, it was a red track he left behind him on the grass and stones. Once, glancing back, he saw the wolf licking his bloody track hungrily. He saw clearly what his own end might be — unless he could kill the wolf. Then began as awful an event as has ever been told; two sick creatures dragging their dying bodies across a wasteland and hunting each other's lives.

Had it been a well wolf, it would not have mattered so much to the man. But the thought of feeding the mouth of that nearly dead thing was hateful. His mind had begun to wander again and he was troubled by hallucinations. His reasonable moments grew shorter.

He was awakened once from a faint sleep by a cough close to his ear. The wolf leaped back, losing its footing and falling in its weakness. It was a funny sight, but he could not laugh. Nor was he afraid. He was too far gone for that. But his mind was for the moment clear, and he lay and considered.

The ship was not more than four miles away. He could see it quite well when he rubbed his eyes. He could also see the white sail of a small boat cutting the water of the shining sea. But he could never drag himself those four miles. He knew that, and was very calm about the fact. He knew that he could not travel another half a mile. And yet he wanted to live. It was unreasonable that he should die after all he had been through. Fate asked too much of him. And, dying, he could not accept death. It was madness, perhaps, but in the very grasp of death he refused to die.

He closed his eyes and tried to keep himself calm. He struggled against the awful desire for sleep that threatened him. It was much like a sea, this deadly sleepiness. It rose and rose, mastering his entire self, bit by bit. Sometimes he was almost lost, swimming through its waters with a weakening effort. Then, by some strange power of the soul, his will would strike out more strongly against it.

Without movement he lay on his back. He could hear, slowly drawing nearer and nearer, the sound of the sick wolf's breathing. It came closer, always closer, and he did not move. It was beside his ear. The dry tongue moved across his face. His hands struck out. Actually, he had willed them to strike out. The fingers were curved, but they closed on empty air. Quickness requires strength, and the man had not his strength.

The quiet waiting of the wolf was awful. The man's waiting was no less awful. For half a day he lay without motion, fighting off sleep. He waited for the thing that was to feed upon him and upon which he wished to feed. Sometimes the sea of sleep rose over him and he dreamed long dreams. But always, through it all, waking and dreaming, he waited for the noisy breath and the feel of the tongue.

This time he did not hear the breath. He slipped slowly from some dream to feel the tongue along his hand. He waited. The teeth passed softly, then more firmly. The wolf was using its last strength in an effort to sink its teeth into the food for which it had waited so long. But the man, too, had waited long. The hand closed on the wolf's mouth. Slowly, while the wolf struggled weakly, the other hand moved across the wolf's body. Five minutes later the whole weight of the man's body was on top of the wolf. The hands had not sufficient strength to grasp the wolf about the throat until it died. But the face of the man was pressed close to the throat of the wolf and the mouth of the man was full of hair. At the end of half an hour the man felt some warm drops of blood in his throat. It was not pleasant. It was like hot, melted metal being forced into his stomach, and it was forced by his will alone. Later the man rolled on his back and slept.

There were some scientists traveling on the fishing ship *Bedford*. From where they stood on the ship, they could see a strange object on the shore. It was moving down the beach toward the water. They were unable to decide what it was. Being men of science, they climbed into a smaller boat and went ashore to examine it. And they saw something that was alive but which could hardly be called a man. It was blind and did not know what it was doing. Its movements produced little effect. But still it continued to drag itself across the ground at the rate of about twenty feet an hour.

Three weeks later the man lay in a bed, on the fishing boat. With tears streaming down his face, he told who he was and what he had experienced. He also talked without meaning about his mother, and a home in California among the flowers.

The days were not many after that when he sat at table with the scientists and the ship's officers. He delighted in the sight of so much food and watched it carefully as it went into the mouths of others. With the disappearace of each mouthful an expression of sorrow came into his eyes. He was not mad. However, he hated those men at mealtimes. He was afraid that there would not be enough food. He inquired of the cook, the cabin boy, the captain, concerning the food supply. They re-assured him numerous times. But he would not believe them and went into the kitchen to see with his own eyes.

It was noticed that the man was getting fat. He grew bigger each day. The scientists shook their heads and gave their opinions on the problem. They limited the amount of food given to the man at his meals, but still his weight increased.

The seamen smiled. They knew. And when the scientists decided to observe the man, they learned the reason. They saw him walk about the ship after breakfast. Like a man begging with an outstretched hand, he approached a seaman. The seaman smiled and gave him a piece of bread. He grasped it, and looked at it as a greedy man looks at gold. Then he put it inside his shirt. He received similar gifts from other smiling seamen.

The scientists were careful. They allowed him to continue. But they secretly examined his bed. It was lined with bread; every inch of space was filled with bread. Yet he was not mad. He was preparing for another possible famine — that was all. He would recover from it, the scientists said. And he did, even before the *Bedford* sailed into San Francisco Bay.

COMPREHENSION QUESTIONS

EXERCISE 1 For each question, write down the letter that corresponds to the right answer. Choose only one.

1 When the man fell from weakness, what did he find to eat?
   (a) Four small birds.
   (b) Four birds eggs.
   (c) A bird with a broken wing.
   (d) Some muskeg berries.

2 Why did it not seem important that he could not find the human footprints again the next morning?
   (a) Because Bill was probably dead, anyway.
   (b) Because great hunger was his only concern.
   (c) Because he had grown to hate Bill.
   (d) Because they were heading in the wrong direction.

3 How did he give himself relief from the hallucination he had about his gun?
   (a) By throwing away the gun.
   (b) By forcing himself to understand that it was empty.
   (c) By opening the gun.
   (d) By pretending to fire the imaginary cartridge.

4 What frightened him now more than the fear of death from starvation?
   (a) The fear of insanity.
   (b) The fear of death from wolves.
   (c) The fear of death through bleeding.
   (d) The fear of going blind.

5 What thoughts passed through his mind when he saw the bones of a young caribou?
  (a) Thoughts of life and death, and the pain of living.
  (b) Thoughts of a wish to die.
  (c) Thoughts of Bill and the loneliness he felt.
  (d) Thoughts of the gold he had thrown away.

6 What force drove him on?
  (a) His suffering and pain.
  (b) The fact that he was a man.
  (c) His hallucinations and wild dreams.
  (d) The life in him.

7 Why, at first, was he unexcited by the sight of the river, the sea, and the ship?
  (a) Because he remembered them from his map.
  (b) Because he had expected to see them.
  (c) Because he no longer cared about anything.
  (d) Because he thought they came from a trick of his mind.

8 Why did he bind his feet with the legs of his trousers?
  (a) Because he had used up his blankets.
  (b) Because in the warm sunlight he didn't need trousers.
  (c) Because soon he hoped to have new clothing.
  (d) Because despite the sun his feet were cold.

9 How does the author describe the way the man walked?
  (a) Like the sick wolf behind him.
  (b) Like a man on his hands and knees.
  (c) Like a dying man.
  (d) Like a baby learning to walk.

10 Why was the sick wolf following him?
  (a) It hoped he would throw away som_ ood.
  (b) It hoped he would feed it some caribou bones.
  (c) It hoped he would protect it against other wolves.
  (d) It hoped he would die first.

11 Because the life in the man refused to die, he continued to do three of the following things. Which did he not do?
  (a) He ate berries and small fish.
  (b) He threw stones at the sick wolf following him.
  (c) He kept a careful eye on the sick wolf.
  (d) He drank hot water.

12 How did he know that the bones which he found were
   Bill's?
   (a) Because no one else was in that region.
   (b) He didn't.
   (c) He found some of Bill's clothing.
   (d) He found a moose-skin bag like his own.

13 What did the man believe Bill would have done had their
   situations been exchanged?
   (a) He would have behaved no differently.
   (b) He would have taken the gold but left the bones.
   (c) He would have eaten the bones and taken the gold.
   (d) He would have eaten the bones but not taken the gold.

14 How far did the man go towards the ship each day?
   (a) Three miles.
   (b) Seven miles.
   (c) One mile.
   (d) Less and less.

15 In what way did fate seem to be asking too much of him?
   (a) He was close to being saved and had suffered too
       much.
   (b) He should not have to die to feed a sick wolf.
   (c) God should not play with him.
   (d) He should not have to die after so much suffering.

16 When the man felt the dry tongue of the wolf move across
   his face, what did he do?
   (a) He struck the wolf in the face.
   (b) He tried, but lacked the strength to grasp the wolf.
   (c) He curved his body and swung away from the animal.
   (d) He struck out powerfully against the animal.

17 What was the most difficult task he now had to do?
   (a) To smell the wolf's breath without becoming sick.
   (b) To move the remaining four miles to the ship.
   (c) To lie without motion when he wanted to strike out.
   (d) To fight off the sleep that rose like a sea around him.

18 Why did the man move his body on top of the wolf?
   (a) Because his hands were too weak to strangle the
       animal.
   (b) Because he was afraid that it might otherwise run away.

(c) Because he needed the warmth from the wolf's body.
(d) Because he could not otherwise remove his hand from the wolf's mouth.

19 When the man felt the wolf's blood in his mouth, how did he react to it?
(a) He drank it hungrily.
(b) The hot liquid felt comforting in his stomach.
(c) He disliked it and had to force himself to drink it.
(d) He tried to drink it but could not.

20 When the scientists from the ship found the man on the beach, what was his condition?
(a) He could no longer move.
(b) He tried to bite them because of his hunger.
(c) He did not know what he was doing and was blind.
(d) He was almost dead and tried to smile at them.

21 When the amount of food given to the man was limited at meal-times, why did he continue to get fat?
(a) Because he still ate too much at the dining table.
(b) Because the seamen were giving him bread between meals.
(c) Because he visited the kitchen numerous times.
(d) Because after going without food, all food seemed to make him gain weight.

QUESTIONS FOR DISCUSSION AND WRITING PRACTICE

EXERCISE 2 The following questions may be used for classroom discussion, for written homework, or for both.

1 Describe what the man did with his bag of gold dust. Why did he do this?

2 What hallucination troubled the man?

3 Describe his encounter with the bear.

4 What thought did the sight of the animal bones produce in his mind?

5 Why does the author say that, as a man, he no longer struggled?

6 When he saw the ship, where was the man, and how did he know this?

7 Why did the wolf near him not attack him immediately?

8 In what way did he consider himself superior to Bill?

9 Describe the man's final struggle with the wolf.

10 What was his condition when the scientists found him?

11 Why did he grow fat on the fishing boat?

12 Do you think that "Love of Life" was a good name for this story?

SYNONYMS

EXERCISE 3 For each question, write down the letter that corresponds to the correct synonym for the word(s) in italics.

1 He ate the four little birds *greedily*.
   (a) cruelly (b) vulgarly (c) hungry (d) eagerly

2 A *hallucination* that he had one cartridge in his gun began to trouble him.
   (a) belief (b) delusion (c) suspicion (d) madness

3 The bear moved away to one side with a *threatening* noise.
   (a) dangerous (b) menacing (c) bold (d) murderous

4 Then the man *yielded* to a fit of trembling and sank to his knees.
   (a) submitted (b) produced (c) reacted (d) suffered

5 Was this life? A *fleeting* thing without meaning?
   (a) running (b) escaping (c) quickly (d) transitory

6 The *unfamiliarity* of the river puzzled him.
   (a) strangeness (b) unfriendliness (c) ignorance (d) unknown

7 It was like hot, melted metal being forced into his stomach, and it was forced by his *will* alone.
   (a) determination (b) desire (c) control (d) independence

8 He *inquired of* the cook, the cabin boy, the captain, concerning the food supply.
   (a) investigation (b) questioned (c) demanded (d) asking

9 The scientists *limited* the amount of food given to the man at his meals.
   (a) lessened (b) measured (c) restricted (d) denied

10 When the scientists decided to *observe* the man, they learned the reason for his increase in weight.
   (a) analyze (b) stare (c) watch (d) take care of

WORD STUDY

EXERCISE 4 Study these words and the sentences that follow them. If possible, repeat them after your teacher. The word in italics in the table is the form found in your reading.

WORD CHART

	ADJECTIVE	NOUN	VERB	ADVERB
1	satisfied, satisfactory, unsatisfactory	satisfaction, dissatisfaction	*satisfy*	satisfactorily, unsatisfactorily
2	hungry	*hunger*	hunger	hungrily
3	curious	*curiosity*		curiously
4	steady, *unsteady,* steadfast	steadiness	steady	steadily, steadfastly
5	quick	*quickness*	quicken	quickly

1 The little birds had not *satisfied* his hunger. Weeks had passed since he had enjoyed the *satisfied* feeling in his stomach of a full meal. A meal of tiny birds was hardly *satisfactory* for a starving man. In fact, small living birds made a very *unsatisfactory* meal, but were better than starvation. He had almost forgotten the *satisfaction* of eating all could comfortably hold. His *dissatisfactions* now were numerous: his hunger, his loneliness, his physical suffering, his loss of direction. Because of his hunger, his brain now worked *unsatisfactorily*. For the same reason he could not sleep *satisfactorily* at night.

2 His *hunger* drove him on. Sleeping and awake, he was constantly *hungry*. He *hungered* for some solid, satisfying food. He chewed on the young caribou bones *hungrily*.

3 The great brown bear was studying him with *curiosity*. It stared at him *curiously*. The bear was *curious* about this strange two-legged creature.

4 His steps were *unsteady,* as were the steps of the wolf behind him. And his tired heart had lost its *steady* beat. The only thing that remained *steadfast* was his will to live. This drive to live made him move on *steadfastly* day and night. When he stood to face the bear, he had to *steady* himself so that he wouldn't fall. His temporary *steadiness* as he stood facing the bear made the animal turn away. His fear made him stand *steadily* and look the bear in the eye.

5 *Quickness* requires strength, and the man had not his strength. The pounding of his heart *quickened* when the wolf took his hand in its mouth. The man *quickly* grapsed the wolf's mouth as firmly as his weakness would permit. Normally, he had a *quick* strong hand, but now he could barely curl his finger.

Complete each sentence with the correct form of the word given before each sentence. The word given is the form found in your reading. Refer to the word chart if necessary.

1 *satisfy* _____ and boredom with work are frequent complaints of industrial workers in modern societies.

Most students do their work _____ but not brilliantly.

2 *hunger* After a hard football game, the children ate their lunch _____.

When away from home, we often _____ for the kinds of food that we are accustomed to.

3 *curiosity* Dull children are rarely _____.

An old saying: _____ killed the cat.

4 *unsteady* When faced with his wife at the front door, the drunkard _____ himself immediately.

A _____ friend is worth ten acquaintances.

5 *quickness* The young man's pulse _____ when a pretty girl passed him on the street.

A good pickpocket must have a _____ hand.